# Fingerprints of God?

A Mix of Religion, Science, and Language

Edward R. Ward

Copyright © 2014 by Edward R. Ward
All rights reserved.

Published by
Kelmscott Communications
1665 Mallette Road
Aurora, IL 60505

Printed in the U.S.A.

ISBN 978-0-9749989-7-8
Library of Congress Control Number: 2014940659

No part of this publication may be reproduced, stored in a retrieval system, or transmitted, in any form or by any means, electronic, mechanical, photocopying, recording, or otherwise, without the prior written permission of the publisher.

# Introduction

When a few things in the world of science intersect with some items of the spirit, life can become endlessly fascinating. Hegel once remarked that heaven on occasion can be "transplanted to earth below," and St. Ignatius has said, "The earth, like the heavens, narrates the glory of God." We are all well advised to think of some words in Isaiah: "Lift up your eyes and look to the heavens."

Our job on this planet is to look for connections, given that some things can be confusing at a distance, while others are a mystery right in our own mental backyard. We read in the book of Wisdom, "Scarcely do we guess the things on earth, and what is within our grasp we find with difficulty." Science does a good job of telling us how the world is, but not how it should be, and into the mix comes the world of the spirit, which provides yet another way of looking at things. Through it all there is language, Vine Deloria's "first glue that holds people together" (or separates them).

How does one find connections, except by unraveling a few things? One goes slowly, and from the heart. A person can spend a few light-years (a designation of *distance*, not time) in the study of what is "up there" in the skies, as well as about what is "down here" on Earth, as well as "in here" in the human heart. The search is not done in a biblical "twinkling of an eye," and we must take advantage of what Nicholas Rescher calls our "useful inheritance," the ability to use the intellect to probe the world for insights and connections that perhaps some people might never see. And religion, by the way, is all about a unique way to *feel*, is it not?

A while ago I became fascinated with searching for possible answers to Einstein's question, "Does God play dice?" I could not find a suitable answer, so I started to look everywhere, starting with zero, both a number and a symbol, for the "fingerprints" of God (to channel Barbara Bradley Hagerty). I have learned that people find some of those fingerprints in a nearby prayer book, in the chemistry of the moon, and in the guy sitting quietly on the morning train. To borrow a bit from Darwin (who in turn is skillfully channeled by Michael Shermer, among others), "There's grandeur in this view of life, with its several powers." George J. Seidel adds that science puts a person in relation to a relationship, and that relationship can be fascinating. Newton has said that we would be smart to think of God and "his most wise and excellent contrivances." Required reading at the outset might be Lisa Randall's *Knocking on Heaven's Door* (Ecco, 2011).

We walk a fine line herein. On one side, some feel that humans are no different from any other species, while others offer that humans are divinely set aside from the rest of nature. (Both positions are false.) On the linguistic side, I do realize that usage, not etymology, gives meanings, and some issues are "beyond words." Nothing is easy.

Not that we are in this discussion to acquire some earthshaking conclusions, although the scientists in the crowd will always look for results. We may instead be in it for the questions. Those in the legal community already know that the questions shape the evidence, and from the lifting up of the sun in the east (Spanish, *levante*) to it setting in the west (Spanish, *poniente*), we should study science, spirituality, and language(s) in order to do some daily *dis*-covering. The task is to live out some understandings and commitments, not just to conjugate verbs and process numbers.

Charles Dickens mentioned "a whole world with all its greatnesses and littlenesses," and Gerard Manley Hopkins said something about a world "charged with the grandeur of God."

The Endnotes and the Bibliography are large, by intent. In the course of writing this, I have believed that they should indeed be vast and ever-expanding, not unlike the universe itself. Such a universe may reflect Manil Suri's "timeless constellation of ideas that lie beyond."

Let's begin.

Edward R. Ward
Joliet, IL

# I.

Maybe life starts on zero, the tenth digit. An awareness of zero can make room for some issues of importance, especially those involving the interior life. Thomas More used to ask God for "the grace to count the world as nothing," while some people may need what David Wolpe calls *bittul hayesh,* a nullification of the self. Some might want to commit to being occupied with God (Latin, *vacare Deo*), while others may wish to do a type of surrender (Arabic, *islam*) in the process. A few might reference the term kenosis (from Greek, an emptying.) Such things are not difficult to label, but hard to live out, no matter the language or the tradition.

However, human beings (frequently indivisible and often unpredictable) are made aware of a different state of affairs daily in America: one should consume and consume, and thereby move away from the integers immediately above zero. The more goods accumulated, the greater the numbers, of course. Numbers are "a plurality of units,"[1] although building up ever-increasing numbers can cause a blocking (Greek, *skandalon*) to the spiritual life. So much for having to process "the messy contents of human history,"[2] like confronting hunger in the life of a stranger, facing an incurable illness in the life of a loved one, or losing a week's wages in a flash at the gaming tables. These things are a far cry from some advice found in the Bible, "Sell everything you have."

Billboards (without number) devoted to casinos (without number) announce the joys of accumulating points, although at a cost, and print advertising urges the advantages of half-off sales, two-for-one transactions, and attractive jackpots. (One must flee from zero!) Numbers, after all, "give a body to things."[3] Such a body is very much measurable, and provides a

*1*

certain "proofiness," to use Charles Seife, for people eager to show off their ability to accumulate. Instant gratification is too slow, furthermore, and the desire to gather is so powerful that it has, in a phrase, almost everyone's number. Who does not believe that combining a bit of math and some consuming does not improve one's life? We are reminded of that *umpteen* times a day. What upper-class person would believe that "legible clothing" (e.g., Aéropostale or American Eagle Outfitters) is a good idea? Who, moreover, wants to perform low-status work to advance up the ladder, when society tells everyone that only the top of the ladder matters? Einstein has said that not everything that can be counted counts, and not everything that counts can be counted, but we accumulate with abandon nevertheless.

Money and impressive numbers do not create character, even with zero down, but money certainly reveals character. It is fine that people make money, but money does not make people; it does not love them back, either. Money is not just a physical thing exactly; its presence can be measured to be in two places (a bank, and en route from it) at one time. Money is so flexible that a person can be, in a phrase, "money ahead" without spending hardly any: washing a car in Syracuse in January can save a person a bucket of money in April by preventing oncoming rust. Money can transform everything—at one moment asking God for a favor (while dropping in a donation in church), and at another buying dangerous fireworks at a location not near home. Brigham Young once said, rather vividly, that gold will sink a man to hell, but many people are willing to risk it. Money, lastly, is "the zero degree of human solidarity."[4] The mention of money at the end of a sentence also puts a powerful exclamation point on the discussion. Notice the silence after someone mentions that two (Club Level) season tickets at the Chicago Blackhawks games for 2014–2015 costs a hefty $13,000. Americans love to spend, not save, and some choose to hoard. (The behavior may be *dis*-graceful.)

The time-space dyad (better, monad) may give way to a time-money confluence in today's consumption-heavy world. Money is a social tool, minimizing risk for those who have money and exposing to risk those who do not. Those with money do their thing with a history "written from records left by the privileged," to use a bit of Howard Zinn. Too few are rich to those in need.

In the world of gaming (formerly gambling), where money and time do a profitable dance, time takes a few interesting turns. The gist for management is to keep people playing and playing, and "in the mood." The attraction for the players is to "make a killing" (not so a strange wording), but at the end of the day management is still feeling the high, the players a low. They mistakenly thought that the high will last forever, and that a fleeting perfection will be achieved. Money is a token (pun intended), and it tends to lose importance as it finishes second to the high produced by the feelings involved. Getting credit becomes the goal, given that same high, even though the losses mount up faster than some can count. Heightened feelings never get old (Latin, *in-vetus*), and some people become inveterate gamblers. Time is little more than the number of hours at work needed to acquire something. In the casinos, luck, mentioned in addition below, has little chance; it is a "lock," not luck, that the house will make money, all else held constant. Those not knowing desire from pleasure will be picked clean, both of their time and their money. The atmosphere is ripe for much *dis*-ease.

It is all about happiness, self-reported and otherwise, as well as fun, is it not? Happiness is after the fact, but fun is during.[5] Somewhat the same with peace and joy; the former is over the long haul, the latter over the short. Further, happy at the start of one's life can lead to making money down the road, not the other way around,[6] although many think that one has to start with money in order to be happy. In addition, if you do start with some money you may be less lonely, and then more wealthy later for the social connections, made easier with that money in the first place. The real mistake may be that the well-to-do think that money will enable a person to sidestep emotional and spiritual "dark nights," since the inner life, to some, can be "a luxury—if not a total waste of time."[7] Did not the folks at Disneyland speak erroneously years ago of being "the happiest place on earth"? Do not the people at Disney work hard today to "create happiness"? (How does one create something instinctual?)

The many words for breath, wind, spirit, and air (a poor conductor of electricity, by the way) may tell us all we need to know about the importance of the interior life, happiness and money aside. The Latin *spiritus* (into Italian, *ispirare*, to inspire, as well as *inspirare*, to breathe in) is well known to Greeks who pick up a pneumatic drill (*pneuma*, air or wind), as they greet Hawaiians with an *aloha* (in the presence of the wind), all of which takes place in an atmosphere (Hindu, *atma*, spirit) of friendship and cooperation. James Jordan adds, perhaps brilliantly, "Breath defines our inferiority"[8] (thinking of human limitations), while scientists discuss how air has a weight to it. Children must change their narratives when parents "get wind" of certain behaviors—parents are thereby aware of the spirit, if not the clear intent, of the kids. Some people fall in love so intensely that they forget how to inhale (Latin, *halare*, to breathe, as in halitosis!). It's all about the wind, er, spirit within us.

The rich, often with ample air under them, have more places for their enjoyment than the not-so-rich, at least in matters external. A second home can do wonders for the human spirit, while the poor exert ownership of very few places, and have limited control of the places that they do inhabit. The rich do not have to sit next to the not-so during sporting events; the rich watch from a soft chair in a warm skybox, while the not-so must sit on metal bleachers. The rich can "buy time" and, when necessary, "go places," while the poor go next to nowhere. Leonard Shlain says that as space contracts, time dilates,[9] and he is right: the walls come in closer, and the clock seems stuck on the present (which is not a gift) for those who cannot afford to move beyond where they are. Garret Keizer charts the proper course when he says much of the rich-poor debate shows vividly what we do not want to admit, that a society can somehow prosper when some are left out. (Hypocrisy weighs more than hedonism.) The group's "moral arithmetic" might be rethought a bit, although numbers tend to define many wealthy people. The rich folks can always afford redemption (from Latin, buying back). Rich in the ways of God is a better stance.

There can be so-called "thin places" for both rich and poor. They are places where heaven and earth seem to come together.[10] Thin places are the places to be if a person finds her life trending downward into "a cosmic lottery," in the words of Os Maguiness. Thin places can tell us that life should not be one's own, but is held "in trust." People who speak Spanish may know that to get anywhere (especially to a thin place) one has to move out of the space (*de espacio*) one is in. Time therein is a distance, not a quantity. (Spanish usually sees time as an amount, but not here.) The word means "slowly," and it yokes both space and time. Thin places are those not instantly visible to outsiders, either. Richard Wolfson widens the discussion by suggesting that places are not just places, but often can be events.

The poor (often nameless in all conversations, as a matter of course) do have more time than rich people, as long as time is not conflated with the ability to effect change. Mathematics and physics people will say that time and change are interchangeable, but the poor may respond that they indeed have the time, but not the ability to change much of anything. (They cannot afford to "buy time" like the rich, either, *ut supra*.) The poor have little of John B. Calhoun's "defensible space," since many people can order them around freely. Poor people sitting outside the local county court house an hour before their court date cannot afford to alter the attitudes and judgments that impact them adversely. A biblical "fullness of time" makes no sense to them. On the contrary, flying in a corporate jet can save a person a lot of money by "making" time, and doing so wearing a luxurious wristwatch (for the rich, a chronometer) is even better. Marshall McLuhan was right: "objects are not contained in space, but they generate their own spaces,"[11] and do so, although awkwardly for the poor. At the end of the day we must say that God sees the poor differently than we do; God does so through the eyes of Jesus. We humans do not. The well-heeled, meanwhile, can buy products that broadcast the elegance of those products to everyone, the poor included. The poor buy products that proclaim very little, except possibly that many of the products do not cost much. Poverty is also a thief—it takes years off a person's life. (Both the poor and the rich confuse comfort with well-being, but such things are best left for another time.)

Leave it to St. Thérèse of Lisieux to move us off a desire to focus our attention on money, alter time a bit, and bolster ourselves. She says that there is indeed a subject that God does not know—arithmetic. God has created, and transcends, the simple numbers of life (one sun, two hands, three divisions of Gaul, four bases) and may not be concerned with issues like how people amass a large quantity of goods. More importantly, does God not tell us that amassing big numbers proves very little?[12] Some people think that if something is expensive (and numerous) it *has* to be good, and we all must rush to do some consuming. Not always and everywhere true.

These points made immediately above are valuable pieces of information, never to be taken lightly.[13] Although information has no color and makes no sound, one must know it when one sees it, and a spiritual life must be equipped for heavy and intimate combat, complete with information that is correct and usable. A few in the spiritual world mistakenly regard facts (aka information for now) to be inessential, but it is better to err on the side of having some facts than to stand and proclaim with only a small care for them. However, a problem may come when we think that information translates easily into knowledge and wisdom, when it often does not. Can we ever discuss the formation of solid values *without* searching for the relevant facts? Bad information, of course, makes for bad spirituality. An important feature of information, whether static or not, is that it does not deplete easily.[14] The same cannot be said of hydrogen

5

or Fermat's Last Theorem. To be avoided at all costs are Uwe Pörksen's "plastic words," items that offer a sweeping sense of everything and a clarity about nothing in particular.

Those who study law ("a profession of words") will mention in a femtosecond that life is not only about what you do; it is also about what you omit, or in some fashion have not had to be involved with.[15] After a number of years, one realizes that it's about what you did <u>not</u> do that is very important. Not dropping out of school and not losing a job now may seem like valued omissions (or avoidances), although central to a fact pattern for success. For good or ill, we know, "we act by contact,"[16] and at times by its absence. It may not be what you do not know that drives your behavior; it is all about what you do not allow yourself to think about, or were fortunate enough in another frame to avoid. Such a perspective dovetails nicely with Robert M. Cover's statement that law involves the projections of an imagined future upon reality... which we can either face or choose not to.

Could life all be a matter of how we lump and split things?[17] We include the Japanese on a list of Asian people, but we tend to exclude the Hmong. On a list of disabled people, we might exclude a woman with cerebral palsy but having a master's degree, but we include a deaf man who excels in tennis. The lumping and splitting may remind us that we either bond with those around us, or we do not. (It is also forever essential to separate the poor from the rich, too, some would argue.) The separating dovetails with the Hebrew word *Ivrim*, to describe people; the word means separation.[18] Church architects know from day one that what is to be made sacred has to be separated, and etymologists would add that Pharisees separate themselves from the various and sundry things around them.

Those who are connected to the people around them should not glibly say, "I know how you feel" when visiting a dying person for possibly the last time. The proverbial (Hindu) elephant is in the room, and so should be the desire to listen, which may be why there are so many words of differing origins connected to sounds and listening: audition, obedience, rehearsal, drone, knell, acoustics, sonic, phonics, etc. One's presence at a bedside (with no regard for the numbers displayed on a clock) carries the day when the person attending the sick or the dying cultivates quietly, to use a bit of Verlyn Klinkenborg, "the feeling of dwelling in a task." Needed, too, is Letty Cottin Pogrebin's "etiquette of honesty," that allows people to tell others with clarity what is felt, what works, and what does not. The visit cannot be done without human feelings (Chinese, *wuqing*), and those feelings must be real, even without the numbers.[19] In such cases we must watch our language, both in listening to someone, and in not speaking about things that do not really matter. Those who know Hebrew know there is *chesed*: to see, think, and feel as another person does. Humans seem to have some choices with their feelings: to repress them, to embrace them, or to divert them.

We must also be willing "to enter into the chaos of another," in the words of Jesuit James F. Keenan. When skies are blue, little guidance is needed, but when skies are even a bit dark, the world shifts. While we all seek Mihaly Csikszentmihalyi's "flow" (a timeless space) we instead often encounter unpredictable interruption after unpredictable interruption. (For women, time is not protected like it is for men.) Unfocused talk and careless listening are the stuff of "dis-*aster*," when the "*aster*-oids" (Greek into usable English, things star-like) are not in alignment.

An important alignment is death, an event, a process, and "the last enemy to be destroyed" in First Corinthians. Death "gives importance and value to time,"[20] and it also performs as a punishment, a gift, a favor, and in some cases was "the supreme sacrifice" (e.g., on Memorial Day). While issues of the liver and the lungs might be fixed by medicine, things like decreasing energy and increasing anxiety (veritable sign posts suggesting the arrival of the final day) cannot be remedied so easily. Is not the worry about dying "the mother of all religions"? It seems it is. Some have to go through what might be called a "bad death," which can be sudden, unexpected, inexplicable, in an ugly place, near the wrong people, etc. This area is one for those who are in touch, with hearts and priorities "in-tact." Tactile, not virtual or viral, works here, all because we have this thing about wanting to be immortal.[21] For the advanced, Seth S. Horowitz says touch involves the "remapping of the mechanical distortion of a structure." Hmm.

Perhaps Einstein never knew that the space-time confluence would advantageously inform people "heading into the sunset." The reference may be temporal, not so much spatial. Red sunsets provide a rubric, affording their viewers an instructive look at a day's final light, as well as a blissful link to an awareness that the Creator makes the light both possible and necessary in the first place. Would that all people could leave this earth with a glimpse of God for just a second or two in the final moments. Science can tell us how we may die, of course, but not exactly how we should live.

Those who are "suddenly single" after the death of a very significant other will understand these things easily. Such a statement will sound hollow to those at Comcast, who tell us all to move "at the speed of necessity." Some, further, may wish to "disindividuate,"[22] focusing on things that will survive a person after her death. Maybe all of us should beg God daily for the "least worst" death, as bioethicist Margaret Pabst Battin would say.

Some in the retailing community want people in darkness. There one cannot "ferret out value."[23] More than a few real estate agents would never show a model house to a prospect amid the dark of night—a potential buyer might see some dark, almost empty, surroundings as well as a good load of inactivity. Certain things are best seen at night when, with occasional anomaly, vision improves. People who sell dresses to women may want to encourage what is black and dark—the wearer, then, does not blend in with the furniture and the drapes.

Daily life was certainly darker years ago, obviously quieter, and possibly more spiritual. The lack of electricity and light, that is to say "administered light"[24] gave people an opportunity for silent reflection, and set the stage for prayer, when necessary. Candles and a lack of electricity provided conditions for a limited darkness, a bit of quiet conversation, and maybe even some contemplation. G. Spencer Brown advises in his <u>Laws of Form</u> that we get both light and a certain wisdom examining the stars, and our minds and hearts may still be in those stars, but others say our destiny now may be in a very different place, our genes.[25] The mention of stars is done about a dozen times in the Qu'rān for at least two reasons: stars erase a certain darkness, of course, and they can articulate the presence of a divine maker. Light is so versatile it can be connected to discovery, warmth, or destruction.

Even the most energetic person does not move through the night as much as travel amid or underneath some darkness. The focus this time is spatial, not temporal. The dark can be a cold and awkward place—a home to uncertainty and fear, although a place of importance. Henry Vaughan, poet, says, "There is in God (some say) a deep but dazzling darkness." One looks straight ahead when walking amid those who are asleep (Greek, *cementerion,* sleeping place) on a cold night in late November. One must fight off incoming impressions of nervousness and doubt, and one must find a home with those things. Helen Keller has said that it is better to walk in the darkness with someone than to walk in the light alone, although some folks prefer to walk alone in the darkness. (Not a good idea.)

We today sing of the stars overhead, with the vision of them being diminished a bit every year due to the powerful lights shining brightly on the earth. A Ph.D. dissertation could be written about the mix of sailors praying that they go "gently into this dark night," and scholars of Dylan Thomas mentioning his "Do not go gentle into that good night." Psalm 139 tells us that those who hide in the darkness, or seek things there, will at some time be illumined—God will catch up.

## II.

By the way, how is it that God is over here, but maybe not so clearly over there, not unlike an electron? We do not know exactly. Not even math, the gold standard of knowledge, can answer that. (God is both within us and beyond us.) We humans should be content to begin with a certain stillness (*nirvana*, free of desire and a blowing out to Buddhists), and go from there.[26] Faith (an acronym: found always in the heart) may help. The spiritual life does not easily and visibly compute its own trajectory subject to "the laws of Nature and Nature's God," to use the Declaration of Independence a bit. God's presence may be more like water, going in no easily predictable direction, and in a type of thickness that reacts with (better, responds to) the forces around it. God used to be found in the nearest mountains centuries ago, but humans have pushed God out, to the margins, of late. Some "sail beyond the sea," says the psalmist, in order to find God's love. With some counter-intuitive thinking, that love may not be so far off.

God loves us, of course, but is importantly hands-off at times in the process. God does not direct auto traffic in Tulsa, and does not rescue a failing engine on an airliner over Salt Lake City. The bottom line may be that God (and his 99 attributes, for those who "believe" in Arabic) loves us far more than we realize, although from a distance. At the end of the day it is not so good to say, "I know God (and His intentions)," and it is much better to say, "God knows me (without myriad conditions imposed by me)." God provides us some space, and even may assign us a place, given some occasional "obscure and afflictive dark waters."[27] To boot, we do not receive a clear and detailed response to much of anything, and maybe we get instead a long and tedious story (Yiddish, *megillah*) that can be difficult to understand. For homework, research the phrase "God from the bottom up" in the work of Jennifer J. Cobb,[28] and then use the term "invisible hand" from Economics 101 in the same sentence.

God, though hidden, seems approachable and hands-on for some, since, they claim, there are fingerprints available, as far as such prints can go. Those prints could be reflected by Steven Curtis Chapman, who once wrote of "a masterpiece that all creation applauds." While God works daily through secondary causes (mentioned above), does anyone know why God is responsible for a person with a baffling genetic disorder? Moreover, how did God create some people with "intrinsic dignity," while at the same time others in that creation are labeled "objectively disordered"? Interesting it is how people believe that God has set up the laws of nature, but is also given the job of intervening in human affairs with frequency.[29] Not easy to be both the cause and the cure. Imagine how tough God has it: there must be a faultless commitment to the truth (and its analogs), and at the same time have the ability to "get it right."[30] Is not much of the physical world as we know it "objectively disordered"? (It certainly can be.) Bible scholars will counter by referencing that God has done some organization "by measure and number and weight."

Whether we think God is hands-on or -off, a man jumped over the edge at Niagara Falls (on the Canadian side) in May, 2012, and it was described as a miracle that he survived. How was that "divine intervention"? How did the person survive? Did God help? How is water not overflowing a container near electricity a miracle? (For the timing, or for the advantageous shape of the container?) Is it a miracle that more people are *not* killed in motor vehicle accidents each month? How are these things an issue of a simple faith, not a series of loosely connected facts? Would it be a miracle for Catholic seminaries to move women, at times supremely accomplished in the classroom, to priestly ordination? The issue is, to sociologists, deeply "embedded," and It would take more effort for the authorities to explain the permissibility of those ordinations than to explain how water should not cross paths with electricity. Maybe we glibly talk in these ways because evil, on the other side, is so strong and is truly "an [opposing] imitation of God."[31] With Einstein's phrase in mind, spooky action at a distance (German, *Spukhafte Fernwirkung*), is it any wonder that some say that God, though a distance away, is what keeps us up at night? Or is it the potential of evil that does so?

*11*

Some feel strongly that they are "good without God,"[32] and more than a few people find the private nature of religion difficult when lived out in public. While some complain of the "cafeteria" style (aka religious relativism) of certain people, there is seldom heard a negative word when such people drop in a donation every week, while not following every word from the pulpit and every law in the catechism. Some put an emphasis on being a good person, as opposed to being the type of person who believes in Jesus, while others abandon going to church, but keep Jesus. (Did not Abraham Lincoln do a variation of this?) Some, further, keep the faith, but lose the local church. Here one may find Marc Prensky's "fallacy of [the] genuine": people may conflate genuine with better, at times ending up on the wrong side of a particular arrangement for a good reason, or the right side for a mysterious reason. A few may be choosing to mimic what a force does physically, at least in the minds of science: they change the velocity and the direction of their lives, albeit with hope.

Atheists, prone to pick and choose like all of us, are happy to explain what they do not believe in, but are unwilling to investigate and own what they say they do not feel. They find a small item of a particular faith, criticize it, and then turn their attention elsewhere. The positive side, to give them their due, is that they say skillfully that some theological "window dressing" should on occasion be dropped in favor of a more relevant narrative. But what is that narrative? Atheist theology, so to say, seems to be one of "a little bit,"[33] and believing "a little bit" may be a down payment, should a severe judgment be rendered one day. Imagine being an atheist and a doctor, reciting the Hippocratic Oath beneath the gaze of "all the gods and goddesses." Further, atheists (about 6 percent) will not put their feelings into music, "the most silent of the arts." The music will stir the mind, the heart, and the soul. In addition, is it not interesting that atheists put their faith in no one, but seemingly have the ability to delineate clearly what and who God is? Of such absences is the atheist position made. They in addition talk of a God in whom very few would want to believe. Last, theists should say more often to atheists, "Disprove it!," but instead atheists challenge theists daily with "Prove it!" and get away with it. Atheists seem to write with invisible ink, while theists tend to enjoy copy machines—distributing texts to unbelievers in order to prove their point. A small number may find some peace in a bit of *Götzengeschwätz* (German, praying to a God whom they do not believe in).

Could not God's activities be in some fashion slightly asynchronic? God, we believe, set up a synchronous rotation of Earth and the moon (showing humans one face only), so why cannot there be some asynchronous activity attributed to God? Internet affairs enjoy asynchronicity: people can personalize their choice of times when they want to connect, without responding to the needs of other people. Jung has warned everyone that the making of things artistic involves some asynchronic behavior; why cannot God so be, or so relate to us? God creates, causes, and observes "across time," but there are moments when there seems to be a delay, kind of like lightning flashing into the view of humans, and then there is the sound, arriving later. The delay may explain why some prayers are not answered in the time frame set up by the person doing the praying. Further, football games on television and radio can be slightly asynchronic. Why cannot prayer, and the answers to it, so be? While photography captures a given moment and keeps it where it found it, people who toil in a library's archives know that what was written in 1805 can, under study, become "now." Time does collapse as well as expand, visible in photographer Mark Ruwedel's eight black-and-white images in the "captured moment" called *Dusk*: decay and decline on one side and development on the other are only a short distance apart.[34] Why should anyone be surprised that a prayer is not immediately answered? It takes light from the sun 8.3 minutes to reach the person reading this paragraph, and it can take hundreds of years for science to move a particular issue "to an adequate conclusion."[35] God gives us life, provides some guidance, and one day will welcome us to a differing place, but the process may seem a short ten years, a painful two years, or a somewhat tranquil six dozen. The catch is both the time and the depth of the involvement.

Some snicker when the suggestion is made that doctors, seldom averse to control, should prescribe prayer along with things like amlodipine besylate, but we must remember that doctors practice, and the practicing can often reference an aspect of commerce, not compassion or empathy so much. Could praying hurt anything? Lawyers and linguists would say off script that there is in such a frame little evidentiality: at times little said to God and little said by God can be found in evidence, even in affairs medical. So, can praying hurt? Stephen L. Carter adds, perhaps loftily, that God "declines to leave the tracks of his existence along the interstices of recorded data."[36] Doctors may say that they indeed measure and measure— but cannot find God. Theists would say that God does what God has to do, and even that "God creates evil, but it is really for our own good,"[37] which may require some praying from the very first day.

Not least, we might have changed the paradigm in some cultures a bit over a few decades, Thomas Kuhn notwithstanding. Way back, the local congregation was the audience, the ministers were the actors, and God (thought at various times to be gold, that is, impervious to change) was the Director. God spoke, people listened, and some were punished (a near-incomprehensible thought today). Now, in a fashion, the congregation is a group of actors, the ministers are the directors, and God is the audience. God hears and sees the whole production these days, from the opening curtain to the final applause, and to bringing up the house lights.[38] In the digital culture of today, however, some make the case that there is no origin in these daily dramas, and not one person is answered to. If God is in the audience, might one ask, "Who writes the reviews?" Hard to say, but if the early reviews are good, the party goes all night. If those reviews are bad, all run home quickly. Maybe there are so many young people who check "none of the above" in religious surveys because of this paradigm shift; Pew Research suggested not long ago that the "nones" have really come into their own in the current religious climate. As the fighting takes place between war and pacifism, pro-life and pro-choice, straight versus gay, the nones (now about 22 percent) move on, feeling fine with what they do and choose not to do along the way. Negative calls the tune.

An adversary (Greek, *satanas*; Arabic, *shaytan*) may be lurking who claims all people and all things are in some fashion equal. The umpire in a game of baseball is impartial, and has the job of spotting activities that make the game unequal, because he himself is to be "uneven" and unequal (Latin, *im-par*). Referees and certain others are commissioned to be *nonpareil* (from French, not equal; Spanish, with awkwardness, *inigualable*) to those nearby, especially to the "fan-addicts" in the stands. Imagine football players of yesteryear throwing Gatorade on Hall of Fame coach Vince Lombardi—he was far from being an equal to his players, and he probably had equality, fairness, and equity nowhere in his mind. There was, by intent, no equal balance (aka equilibrium, from Latin). A priest at a Catholic Mass prays briefly to be washed of his "in-iquity" (Latin, *iniquitas*, unevenness, and also translated inequality) so that for at least a few moments during a particular Mass he can act in the person of Jesus, to whom there is no equal. We knock on wood to channel the triumph of Jesus on a (wooden) cross against any and all adversaries. To Him there is no equal, although certain inequalities in daily life should indeed be celebrated, not rationalized as incorrect (e.g., women in the military). No one should hold God responsible for circumstances that are easily labeled unfair by mere mortals.[39] Those circumstances can have outcomes that can be severe. Complaints and laments should be summarily dismissed, with the will of God never being part of the equation. "No one asked for this" and "It's not fair" should be greeted with a firm counterattack: "Life certainly is not fair, but one has to perform anyway." Life is a gamble, and a gamble is fair if its expected value is zero. (Due to circumstances often uncontrollable, zero is seldom the norm, of course.) Since God is under no obligation to us, we are not owed anything, to be sure. We should *not* feel entitled. When a loved one gets cancer, nothing seems fair. Life for cancer patients becomes a matter of enjoying the small things, and bypassing larger ones. Some who are distant from cancer may not grasp that an "unjust law" may indeed be unfair, but correct as a matter of law. Robert M. Cover expands the discussion by saying that law is "the projection of an imagined future upon reality." Cancer pushes onto people a future that does not have their approval, but must be lived in nevertheless. *Dis*-eases are unfair indeed.

Many will voice, "I do not deserve this." First, deserving can have at best little connection with events and their consequences in real life. Deserving seems vague. An unfocused "You owe me" does not work, or help, either.[40] Such a stance may suggest N. T. Wright's "moral blackmail." Parents should give to their children everything that they need to be successful, including roots and wings, not what they, the parents, somewhat mysteriously think that they, the kids, are entitled to. Did not Hobbes say that life is "nasty, brutish, and short"? This is the turf of "poor-me paranoia,"[41] and this approach cheapens the role of God, if not the will of God, too. (Alibis work that way.) Some will say that rules are not rules; they are only, with possible sarcasm, "entrenched generalizations" in Fred Schauer's words. Do not these attitudes suggest an ideal background for those wishing justification as they go out to get a gun and go on a rampage? They may feel they do not deserve the life they have, and will shout "That does not count," a statement made by innumerate types who display a few issues of control and authority.[42] A good response is, "I have just done some counting, and I can provide a number." New York City employs a director of poverty research, whose job is to count poor people and their conditions (that they do not deserve, we know). If, after all, the world is only "an ocean of increasing misery."[43]

then we can easily make a game out of this odd journey (Arabic, *hajj*). This stance all but guarantees spiritually the inability to breathe (Greek, *a-pnea*), especially for those who display what Michael Kimmel calls "aggrieved entitlement." Some people lead lives that are discrete, not continuous, and to some degree sequentially ordered, but not consequentially related, while certain people spend great energy explaining their lack of involvement.

Those who are innumerate may conflate two things: a person who ministers to other people, and the one who counts differently and is stuck on the self. The former does not want to be the boss, the magistrate (Latin, *magis*, greater), but wants instead to be less (Latin, *minus*, as in minister). Successful outreach accompanies those who are less, indeed those with an eye on downward mobility (like Jesus), not upward. Years ago Catholic religious women consumed daily a can of soup, a piece of day-old bread, and a cup of warmed-over coffee, and that was supper. They understood that to be greater they had to be less (minuscule, if one wills), and they might have been thrilled that others thought less (or little) of them. (And there were plenty of people awaiting the opportunity to "be less" in the convent in those days!) Kind of simple: plus or minus, more or less, to do good or to do well, although some want only to do well, a very narrow set of circumstances.[44]

In all of the above we are known by our mistakes. They define us, although we are schooled to think that many will think us stupid for making them.[45] People feel shame when they err, but maybe the mistakes should be seen as "missed takes," not unlike what a Hollywood filmmaker would reference. Missed takes should not be glibly fastened to shame and blame, or dismissed easily, either, but improved upon. A bright side is that making errors can give people hope—they might feel they can do better in the future, given some past failures that do not crush them.[46] Engineer Henry Petroski would add that success is success, but it is failure that drives the chance for some improvement. We should "fail forward,"[47] improving as we go. Often the best basketball players are the most aggressive ones, and they can commit a large number of fouls. One might add that human error is a part of every game, and a part of life, and can seldom be completely eradicated by technology. The danger is found not in making a mistake; the problem is feeling comfortable with having made a mistake, or making others have to live with our mistakes. Galen Strawson softens the situation a bit by using the term "up-to-me-ness," a term that some may cherish and others will dislike.

Those who truly wish to confront a few serious issues are better off to ask, "Why *not* me?" not just, "Why me?" Why have certain things (e.g., cancer, an early death, emotional vacuums) happened to some people, but not to *me*? Is there a reason why I was excluded? Should I be happy to have been excluded? These may not be easy questions to ask, and we often do not have answers. The questions seem to look for answers beyond the person himself, and a more beneficial stance may be to ask, "How did this happen?" The existential side of the questions cannot be answered so easily; maybe the scientific side can find a bit of an answer. (To be sure, science addresses the how, religion the why, and we are in control of our lives far less than we think.) Such conditions prevail again when we ask, "Why [ ... ] God [ ... ]?" as in "Why did God cause a particular state of affairs, often in a problematic way?" as opposed to "Why, God, did you allow an unpleasant state of affairs to happen to me?" The comma configures an address of the question to a very important person, highlighting the very nature of things in a more intimate and less cognitive way for the questioner. Some instruction (Hebrew, *mitzvah*) is needed, and that instruction (from Latin, *instruere*, to build) must be firm.

A person might wish to pursue another question, "Am I a good (or good enough) person?" The start to an answer may be to ask also, "Am I *not* a good person?" or "Why am I not a worse person?" The questions "ground" the one who asks them; a start may be to examine the blueprint present in all of us since childhood. (Early development in a number of areas is often the key.) In addition, why am I told, "You are not Catholic enough," and why is my neighbor told, "You are very Jewish"? (What is a person to do?) We may realize we are less in control and "less good" than we think ourselves to be.[48]

Behaviors and events that befall each and every human constitute on this "firmament" a physics of social behavior, to channel Alex Pentman a bit. The weight of personal shortcomings and the momentum of daily humdrum make for more work (French, *travail*) certainly, and to soften things one might wish to read a few parables, which etymologically locate people at various places along a given line (Greek, *parabola*). Such an arc helps us to measure ourselves, whether we are, for example, a wasteful people or not. If God is a person who at times challenges, we should recall John Polkinghorne, who argues that God's job is not "to relieve the sweaty discomfort of the believer."[49] God at times confounds us. The burden (Latin, *onus*) is on us to move our masses through potentially difficult distances, possibly with some Christ-like momentum. Jesus died for many (but not for all?), and certainly did not arrange the world for us,[50] or make its physics more intelligible.

The answers to some of the above may hinge on how we do not see ourselves as disabled, although it seems that Jesus of Nazareth might have been. Too often the measuring stick is perfection, as well as the notches immediately below it, and the point is missed: we humans live in a world of "limitation, humility and vulnerability."[51] If all hips and legs functioned well, would we not look at the Son of God in a different way? Being disabled was thought to be a political liability for Franklin Roosevelt years ago; the condition is not seen that way today, especially for those who would not be president. Those who speak Spanish use *minusválido* for a person who is disabled; the word looks like "less valid" or "less valued," while *desvalido* in Spanish means downtrodden, but not devalued. Many disabled people are unfortunately considered little more than their diagnosis. More pointedly, do not many parents disable their children? (Can that be said loudly?) The adjective, disabled, is easily fastened to those with bad legs or defective arms, but is not as frequently used as a verb, describing people who do an insufficient job in a critical area, like parenting. Last, are those seen to be "morbidly obese" not truly handicapped?[52] And is a girl in her late teens who can pole vault, but with considerable deafness, disabled? Often those who are disabled are treated as if they are children, and will always be.

## III.

The negative side of life again seems more vivid than the positive when we return to a favorite question: we ask why God does *not* intervene more often to solve things both personal and corporate? In addition, we ask why God does *not* let good things happen more frequently to good people, and maybe to good people only?[53] Cannot God be (more) active at all times relevant, even if situated in the audience, mentioned above? Roy F. Baumeister talks clearly of "the myth of pure evil,"[54] and Karl Barth underlines that some people, overwhelmed by the prospect of death if not by a difficult life, are "negativized, negated." Richard Rohr says we must fall upward (or, fail forward, according to Peter Simms, mentioned earlier). Athletic coaches constantly think of the losses they've endured, not the wins. Should not God have been helping in all of this? To find fossilized things on Mars may be difficult, but to prove that there are no fossilized things anywhere on Mars is more of a job. The spiritual life may resemble life in the financial world—it is all about managing risk, avoiding failure, and surviving loss. Negative calls the tune, again.

A lot goes through the human heart, which may be why there are so many words in English based on the Latin word for it, *cor*: excoriate, accord, courageous, etc. While certainly engaging the heart, love seems to be a decision, not an emotion. In Arabic, the word *qalb* means both heart and a turning. A heart has to adjust, certainly, and a question may be, "Do we love each other for a set of qualities, not surprisingly, or for a particular person's absolute singularity?"[55] How much do our hearts turn? We might be wise to believe that those whom we love are loaned to us by God, our own so-called "craven" hearts (First Corinthians) notwithstanding, and we

*19*

should instead cultivate a bit of *ren* (Chinese for benevolence) in daily life. One believes with the heart (Romans), and those with a *leb somea* (Hebrew, listening heart) win the day. Did someone say that to desire a person is an issue of regret, a regret of the absence of that person? Maybe it is all meant to be (Yiddish, *bashert*).

Some in leadership positions in the United States, at least, seems to have passed often on their role as parents who look into the heart and have to punish their own. Maybe today's narrative about pedophilia should have included some punishing, as difficult as that may sound. What is a fair and just punishing one can debate, as the argument will be heard often that the punishment must fit the crime,[56] but that is just the beginning. Punishing is embedded: it deals with complex issues of law-making, sentencing, and the administration of penalties. Not easy. Nor is it easy to understand why we insufficiently punish those in the suite, but punish excessively those on the street.[57] Not least, punishment is located in the arena of emotion, not intellect; it is more difficult to handle. There are many questions: where is the line between motivating and abusing? Are strong punishments to be balanced against commensurately powerful rewards? Does not the law have a kind of violence intrinsic to it that we may not want to get into? Should not the punishment be proportional to the harm caused, at the least?[58] (Is the story of the Prodigal Son a tale of forgiving or punishing?) Maybe we fear this process because we think we will get the whole thing wrong.[59] Too bad the punishing has not been done with what the first archbishop of Chicago, Patrick Feehan, mentioned in 1893: [a] "clear and correct conscience."

All we need is love, we all sing, but love can also be God.[60] In good times, experiences are aggregated, and the world seems "love-ly." Everything seems to come together, and when in love the world's size, secondly, does not frighten us so much. Further, love is "additive, not detractive."[61] Love, like God, seems to choose us; we may not in an obvious way choose it. Circumstances frequently beyond our control and understanding come together and voilà, something very nice happens. Planning it all out may be insane; both poets and theologians have told us so for centuries. Gregory Baum, as a caution, has said that the more we believe that God is love, the more difficult we may find it to believe in God: it is hard to love a God in a world both confusing, spiteful, and iffy. Love, however, can become twisted, and can lead to Michael Miller's "intimate terrorism," the manipulation of one person by another in the worst of interpersonal ways.[62] Such things have been true for ages (aka eons, from Latin/Greek). Terry Tempest Williams adds insightfully that if a man knew what it was (or is) that a woman will never forget he'd love her a lot differently.

Someone should write a book detailing how a person in certain circumstances should know how to face certain internal desires and inclinations in order *not* to love another person. While feeling a strong attraction or two is permitted, a few things have to be respected and obeyed, given certain obligations and agreements, often tacit. (We wish to be loved for the same reasons that we love ourselves.) Marriages and other encounters are made (or not made) in the unconscious: much of falling in love never makes it to the surface, although superficial things do. This trip about not loving goes through the doors of privacy and a treasured and measured secrecy: where one person starts and ends goes hand in hand with where another person starts and ends, and how much is revealed about particular impulses and desires must be weighed carefully. Much turns on trust and its radius. Another step should involve prayer, although praying to God that certain feelings go away is not a good idea. Prayer, the "royal road" according to Pope Francis, may be defined as a person's desire to allow God to love the person doing the praying, while a concomitant wisdom may include the grace to know what to do when a person does not know what to do, to say nothing of the ability to understand what moments and motions are foolish (Latin, *fatuus*, as in infatuation). One help may be cultivating the ability to dream, but not to do. It is called falling in love for a reason (we are losing some control, but gaining a bit nevertheless), and falling out of love (we must live with possible loss) may not be a bad thing. Oliver Burkeman mentions "an oblique stance toward one's own inner life," a negative capability. Falling in love and falling apart may not be far from each other. Through it all, a person should somehow learn how <u>not</u> to say glibly "I love you" in certain time-appropriate circumstances.

Both living and loving involve occasional lightning. The lightning one sees in the sky is reminiscent of the personal fireworks that people experience on occasion on the inside. Those who study "inner space" already know that physicists to this day debate the origins of fulminating in outer space. Plato spoke, appropriately, of "lightning and other such visitation of God." Robert L. Wolke tells us that air is a poor conductor of electricity,[63] while Ben Franklin in 1752 knew that the flash (a "universal blow" to him) is seen before the sound is heard, and he might have been thinking of (inter)personal relations. Biblically, thunder is "the voice from heaven," and one can also read about "fire from heaven." The data in the sky precede the construction of a narrative on the ground. In a practical way, significant talking must follow the roar; great times will happen "in the telling." Lightning benefits Earth in a physical way, and in another sense, who has not gone through the lightning of a divorce, an addiction, or an unfortunate distancing from a loved one? Is there not significant growth thereby? Some feel that van Gogh's *Starry Night* (June 1889) might have resulted from electric storms in the artist's brain. (Some epilepsy?) Where else to get the whirlpools of stars?

Grief (French, *chagrin*) is important. It goes with separation anxiety and mourning, and the two may be one reality (Greek, *hendiadys*, one through two, like honor and glory, vim and vigor). We grieve, and in comes some depression, too, in the same motion, as the parameters of grief and depression are still hotly debated. Rare is the life that is spent without some combination thereof. D. H. Lawrence spoke of "the dark vast forest" within each person. It seems like just yesterday when society tried to shield young people from grief, especially in the case of the death of a loved one, since death and life were thought to be opposites. A grief-free life is indeed difficult, and probably not worth living. Depression makes a striking appearance when doctors reference the collision of nouns in "morbidity depression," not unlike the mix of adjectives in "morbid obese," more and more a problem that morphs into a disease. Elizabeth Lunbeck uses "morbid dependency." Morbid is not too strong a word on the heels of grief: morbid connects with the Latin *mors* (death), just like the linguistic connection with the "dying off" of a debt, a *mort*-gage. Depression can in fact be repression, too, of course.

Gravity ("more of a nuisance than a law," and the weakest force) both pushes and pulls, to channel Einstein, and the heaviness of one's life drives an individual to do what has to be done, at times against one's better judgment. Terry D. Cooper channels psychologist Karen Horney when he talks of the loss of a person's "center of gravity,"[64] and we also know, "Gravity, like God, touches every piece of creation."[65] Gravity monitors apples that do some falling and planets that keep their distance. Even further, the scientific community has told us that gravity and pressure are related.[66] People feel a force (with both magnitude and direction) on a Metrolink train coursing through St. Louis daily, not unlike a soft nudge from God. Simone Weil talks of two forces, gravity and grace, with reason; one pushes and the other gathers,[67] and Herbert Butterfield mentions, "that gravitational pull in human nature, which draws the highest things downwards, [and] mixes them with earth and treats them with human cupidity."[68] Both science and religion are forever looking for the Standard Model (or Theory of Everything), push, pull, and gathering included.

Geometry, someone said? The study of form, not quantity? It is a beautiful thing, and is everywhere, from churches in Europe to music, to science, to urban planning, to quilting, and to the spiritual life.[69] The geometry of our lives has a shape (often framed by jobs and must-dos), a few angles (itinerant sickness, a possibility of divorce), and even some tri-angles (loving ourselves, others, and the dangers therein). We know, "Geometry was God's language"[70] and geometry is "number in space."[71] Blaise Pascal, a veritable hero to science people at least, once remarked how geometry was useless. He was wrong. Kepler was also wrong to think that a geometric cosmology was the only one around.

In our own cosmologies we wonder about some closure to things. Frequently there is none.[72] Some wish closure on an issue like pedophilia; there is none.[73] There was no closure on some racial affairs almost a century ago, when some thought that certain people had only to die and take their memories with them. Closure's bibliography, not least, is indeed large.[74] Further, some would have us believe that physical changes make all things in a particular building new, and can change memories and therefore close things.[75] In all of the above there is the danger that things may get out in the open, "transformed in the telling," and there may be little *dis*-closure (Greek, *apokalypsis*). Is not closure proceeding with difficulty in Newtown, Connecticut these days?

The movement of sound and light can manifest itself in magic, which is about "the linking of a cause with an effect that has no basis in physical reality but that—in our hearts—ought to."[76] Priests and ministers know something about this, since from Persian into Romance languages comes priest first, then magician (*magos* in Spanish, at least.[77]) God knows that there are all kinds of sorcery and fetishes out there, to say nothing of "rattles, amulets, herbs, and incantations."[78] Magic can give humans a sense of control, so the gist may be not to extinguish magic and magical thinking, but to "harness" it.[79] Magic is an expression, says Wittgenstein. It speaks of realities (e.g., human knowing and its workings) that we should be familiar with.

Luck and chance are also important. Luck (if one wills, probability) might have been a lady to Frank Sinatra, but it is "a conspiracy of random and minor factors," to use a bit of Leonard Mlodinow. Basketball coaches reference the sentence, "At times it is better to be lucky than good." Chance, for its part, is a short walk away, and it has to do with probability again. We speak of a "chance encounter." Imagine the quizzical looks on the face if one were to say, "I encountered God by chance," and more mysteriously, "God encountered me by chance." (What is chance's definition then?) The previous mention of what a miracle is may somehow dovetail nicely with an inclusion of luck and chance.

Much of life turns on memory, especially when it intersects with loss aversion. Life begins at zero (or conception), and in the younger years it is all about calculating what one can live with and what one can afford to live without, car buying, mate selection, and God included. Success is measured one pebble (Latin, *calculus*) at a time. Whether at zero (the homeless? the friendless?) or at 90 out of 100 (friends without number?), life is all about laboring to avoid loss(es).[80] It is not about the high numbers one has recorded in the quiver; it is about remembering how to avoid losses. Some at the end of their lives have remaining only about 10 percent (Latin, *decem*, as in decimated).[81] Most will have to remember what choice theorists call ambiguous loss: we are glad to have had certain resources and some special people in our lives, but going forward will not at all be the same *sans* those significant resources and people.

Memory, often working best when connected to emotion, moves on its own, a fact known all too well to those who have loved ones with some issues of loss of memory (Greek, *a-mnesia*). Many are forced to wonder if their significant other must fall in love with them all over again, a frightening prospect. Some are able to find their way back, while others cannot. Théodule Ribot in 1881 reminded everyone that memory leans forward (French, *en avant*) and glances backward (French, *en arrière*), and we know that the oldest memories are "the first to return, memory loss shrinking from earlier to later."[82] A person might today remember the batting average of Ted Williams in 1941 (.406), while forgetting yesterday's need to pay the light bill. Veteran college basketball fans in Terre Haute, Indiana use their memories today to channel the games when Larry Bird of Indiana State University was lighting up the skies in early 1979, but the current students have no such memories, and they do not show up in great numbers for the games.

Today's Alzheimer's patients sometimes freeze the age of a 50-year old who visits at 30, say, and the visitor has to deal with it. Patients can end the day not knowing who they are and, in a Pauline sense, *whose* they are: they cannot begin to realize that we humans are not our own, but someone else's.[83] Lost, too, is Kurt Goldstein's "abstract capacity," the ability to perform some routine tasks, but not the ability that requires the formation of a judgment (or two) in the process leading up to the routine task. A person can take out the garbage by rote, but not establish at other times the fact pattern necessary to start that process. This story is written in what some might call the permanent present tense, and the run-up to the activity is the important part, not the results so much.

We all want to memorialize ourselves in some way or another, given our focus on ourselves one day dying, which may be why horror movies featuring people who rise from the dead will always be with us. It is also all about a desire to manage our lives up to the final hour and beyond, and being able to say goodbye meaningfully to others. For homework, converse with friends about how content drives technique, and how form follows function. (Science says that theory determines what can be observed. Discuss.) What we wish to do (be remembered?) frames how we go about doing it.

Of course, *not* having the ability to store certain items in the memory may be a good thing, too.[84] While our memory is more powerful than computer memory, although slower, we know that in the working years (admittedly a wide definition) failed job interviews, inappropriate love affairs, and messed up plans of whatever nature are maybe forgotten by some, or let go of, albeit with a need for forgiveness. Some let go, while others let God. To lift some words from a few Catholic bishops in 1852, all of us should persevere "through the bowels of the mercy of God" to cultivate a mind and a memory that enjoy the greatest thing on earth—a pleasant blend of productivity and longevity. Maybe it is better to live a somewhat forgetful and altruistic life, and, with a pun, have little to show for it,[85] than to have to deal with the ups and downs of being pulled and pushed by credits and debits driven by memory and its movements. Nicholas Delbanco would reference "lastingness."

Things like buying (and buying often) require that we are active, "forgetting truth and believing a falsehood."[86] In order to buy (and buy anew) we have to forget the old product or service, and purchase one that is, of course, new and improved. Fortunes turn on memory, or its absence. Aleida Assman and Jean-François Lyotard would add the terms "memorycide" and "dememorization." "Collective forgetting" may be a good thing, too.

The forgetting, away from its role mentioned earlier in retailing, can be tied to the need to forgive, which should be part and parcel of every moral person's life. While some may question if forgiveness "resets both scores to zero,"[87] there is little point in saying, "I can forgive everyone but myself." One can indeed forgive oneself, and reconciliation (Latin, *cilia*, eyebrows) takes place eye to eye; one must look others in the eye.[88] Should not everyone learn to admit that a wrong done was indeed wrong?[89] For the record, God is both forgiving and kind in the Qu'rān, while Alfred North Whitehead, for his part, uses "tender" to describe God. Forgiveness is much greater than the sum of its parts.

Life involves shadows, called "light's negative traces," and they are not easy to deal with. They have no mass, and while the speed of light is one thing, the presence of a shadow (that is, of *nothing*) is quite another. As a reminder, the speed of light governs what is, not what is not. A person is wise to say that the light of knowledge must be set against the "soft side" of shadows. Shadows are like water; they "seep" into the most unlikely places, even onto the 8x11 paper under the lid of a duplicating machine left slightly open. Photographers know that shadows can be a presence, not just an object, and shadows are not infrequently gendered feminine (and intuitive), *yin* in a (Chinese) word. The shadows are to be governed by what is strong, substantial (and rational), *yang* in a (Chinese) word. The shadows may get the last laugh for reasons connected to Jung—the brighter the light in one's life, the greater the shadow(s). Ask anyone in politics or professional sports. Wise is the person bold enough to confront her own personal shadows, while intelligent enough to seek the comfort of some shade on a brutally hot day.[90]

Shadows can refer to a limitless number of things. A shadow can be what is slight or small or almost without substance, without a shadow of delay (French, *sans l'ombre d'un retard*) in the aforementioned Thérèse. Myles Coverdale, a force in the sixteenth century, is a bit more heavy, using "in the shadow of the valley of death," and the Psalms speak of "the shadow of your wings." Knowing that there is a ray of hope near the shadows may get a few people through some difficulties. Robert Axelrod says correctly that we all live in the shadow of the future. Living in the subjunctive mood is not a bad thing, either. Would that everyone might realize that.

# IV.

An option can be a desire to live in the passive voice, but such a stance may not be a great idea. Some issue to God a gentle and well-known command with frequency, "Be it done to me according to thy will," while others will wish to be more active, if not proactive. To be avoided is "learned helplessness," a term familiar to both Martin Seligman and Dalton Conley,[91] as well as "terminal helplessness," a wording known to Wilfred Graham. Christopher Hitchens spoke before his own death that he was "dissolving in powerlessness like a sugar lump in water." Some do not want to live, and more than a few do not want to be kept alive. Eduardo Bonilla-Silva says using the passive voice enables easy mislocations of both praise and blame. (An American "racism without racists," he claims, can result.) Passivity's up side is that it may translate somehow into an eventual stillness that may let God in to do some things.

Hearing is important, though some do not hear because they are not looking in the right place(s), for hearing and looking are connected. One cannot hear what God is saying if one's eyes are on personal gains, loss aversion, and buyer's remorse, for example. Countless fortunes have been lost for people not listening. Were people listening during the days preceding the attacks in New York on 9-11 a few years ago? (A woman is allowed to be speech-less and not hearing when receiving a diamond ring for the first time, of course.) Jung reminds us that those who are "full" of fear often seek out noise to scare away what they do not want to hear. Those not hearing, as well as those unwilling to listen, are advised to learn of Nelle Morton's "hearing the silence into speech."

A posture of silence is often underestimated since it intersects with noise. Noise, for the record, is "the fine print in our contract with the world,"[92] and that contract is important because it may contain terms that are not justified.[93] We exchange noise for quiet, but maybe the price in the contract is too high. We also want to talk to God in said quiet, but maybe God is in some fashion unavailable. Ralph Ellison is right: we should live in the music of life and refuse to die with the noise. Noise involves just too many things: subjectivity, objectivity, many definitions, etc. And maybe there is occasional silence of a delicate nature, as in a divorce "narrative," when there are very few meaningful words to say. Period. St. Thérèse says, "God instructs without the noise of words."

Maintaining silence takes work, just like keeping secrets does. St. Benedict protests about "empty imaginings and cruel commentaries," although some social scientists may see an upside to a small amount of conversation. It can bind people together.[94] David Wolpe mentions, "Silence is a symphony."[95] He is right, and so is Karl Rahner, who tells us that all symphonies remain unfinished. Gustav Mahler, furthermore, is also correct to claim that a symphony must contain everything, including some well-placed silence. Pope Benedict XVI has added that we are to be "filled" with silence. He would know the meaning of *muta praedicatio* (from Latin, silent preaching), whereby actions do the talking, and the silence is not just along for the ride. Lawyer Marianne Constable speaks of the silence of the law: life can be fine without a deluge of words, but it requires significant work.

Silence and tears easily intersect. We tend to go silent when we cry, and tears signify "the fragility of the human heart."[96] In those tears, which produce blurred vision every time, we contemplate our own "forced errors," tennis players' language for moments that focus on an event that changes the course of the match and "undoes the world."[97] The tears often arrive as a breakthrough, when a person is serious about facing a few things, and are a part of Catholic theology.[98] St. Benedict barred loud display of emotion, curiously, but not tears. A few ancient cultures, like the Olmec people in Mexico, have one word for both rain and tears. People in Evansville, Indiana remember December 13, 1977, "the night it rained tears," when the plane crashed that was carrying the men's basketball team from the University of Evansville. The Bible knows something about these things, reminding readers that those who sow in tears will reap rejoicing.

Silence goes well in a monastery, based on the Greek *monos* (only and alone). *Only* certain behaviors are allowed to an individual in a monastery as she goes to her cell and dwells there, *alone*. Such people live alone (Spanish, *solo*) and are allowed only (Spanish, *sólo*) certain behaviors. (The differing written forms do not matter that much for the moment.) A narrow line herein exists between what is one's own, is a single activity, and pertains to the individual (*privus* in Latin), as opposed to what a person is deprived of (*privatus*). Some find success (again) with St. Benedict's *claustra* in Latin, "monastic enclosure and stability." Being alone goes well when we contemplate a few issues of science as well as religion, like how a place such as Carl Sagan's pale blue dot has had so many things go right for it to exist, when other planets have not.[99] (By the way, are privacy and loneliness the same thing? Seems not, although they may look identical to some.)

Silence is much greater than the absence of sound, or the effects of turning the sound off. Silence can dominate when speakers of a particular language suddenly realize their talk is being understood by an "outsider." Silence is created by the feeling that there is something to be lost in the transaction, or that sharing might not be the best way to go. (Are there not some important analogues of this in the world of the visual arts?) Silence can tell a person all she wants to know, and it can be used to say nothing (which can be something), especially when confronting a reality as difficult as an approaching death. Silence may be a measurable and noticeable punctuation mark in a given conversation, allowing participants to do some contemplative measuring. Would that all people could embrace silence enough to recognize the voice of God "in a gentle breeze," as did the prophet Elijah.

One person's silence can be another's hearing loss. Some unknowingly confuse the two, and what can seem to be a foray into the world of silence may more accurately be a trip into a world of cognitive problems. A concomitant and exaggerated sense of privacy, secrecy, and frustration (and anonymity?) might also set in, releasing feelings both in the local "family" and in the individual that are hard to cope with. Those into the spirit must hear like a blind person does: in time, in darkness, without notation, and in a space where actions and practices can be controlled. Is there not great meaning in "The Lord hears the cries of the poor"? Thomas Keating, a member of the Trappists, once remarked that silence is the language that God speaks, and all else is a bad translation. There are reasons why in St. Benedict's <u>Rule</u> one starts with an encouragement to listen (Latin, *Obsculta*).

One might ask, "Why is God silent when a person doing some praying feels that God is needed most?" Pierre de Locht adds that God often seems the most silent when a possible death encroaches,[100] and humans need both a voice and some instruction when loved ones pass away. Maybe God is silent because others are talking too loudly at the same time. There may be habituation here: God is indeed talking, but pounding noises drown out everything, and humans become distracted by the noise of the pounding. Or, are listeners themselves legitimately too busy to hear what is being said? By the way, does God speak with significance to old, defective ears as much and as often to young, well-functioning ones?

Maybe those who pray are saying silently some intelligible words, but do not truly speak a particular language. Teachers of World Languages (formerly Foreign Languages) instruct about blending sounds and words in response to others: some can easily repeat these days, "My house is blue" and maybe even "Your house is green," after seeing a picture of one, but that is not exactly speaking a language. There is no "processing" there. Speaking a language and putting correct words back to back require more than a devotion to a concordant style and some "facticity."[101] What does one do if the question becomes, "Is there adequate financing on your gray house?" Praying may work the same way: sending things heavenward is one thing, but integrating words and behaviors in the here and now may be quite another. We should not talk to God as much as listen for God. Abraham Heschel has said insightfully that God does indeed speak to us, but does so one syllable at a time. We should not pray that God will at long last hear us, but in order that we will soon hear God.

Of course, there has always been a time when some people claim to be listening *to* God as well as speaking *for* God. Prophets, seers, and intermediaries are always available (to just about anyone who will listen). (Foucault reminds us that speech both says and does.) Lawyers may ask, "Who makes the rules that frame the rules?"[102] Scientists, meanwhile, may interject, *à la* Paul Davies, "Does every event have [to have] a cause?" Listening brings a lot with it.

In our silence we know that Carolyn G. Heilbrun advises that much of life must pass through the gates of gender, listening included. Women are often reduced to zero in various relationships, languishing in "a lifetime of marginality"[103] and silence, as men watch their stars ascend, with concomitant accolades and dollars. Women are often made immobile, stuck on zero, or on a number near it, as men increase their numbers and move about. Women may get hysterical (Greek, *hystera*, womb), but the fear may not be firmly grounded: more recently the biology of women is no longer their destiny, while female biology can indeed be male destiny.[104] It can be a woman's world, and men have a *lot* to lose if and when they "visit" a woman in a certain fashion with outcomes that have serious ramifications for both. Marilyn Frye adds, "[the] voice of the men's world story is the voice of the speaker who does not have to fit his words into the truth, because the truth will fit his words." Many women seek to lose none of their autonomy, listening (again) included. Heilbrun also mentions that the sign of a good arrangement between two people is that *all* things are debatable and can be challenged.[105] Men, meanwhile, think they are experts about the female body, the divine form, and think they can fix everything. (They cannot.) We've come a long way since the days when a woman was what some others said that she was, *la femelle de l'homme* (from French, the female of the man).

It can be a pleasant etymological walk from living a simple lifestyle (not far from zero) to existing in something of a vacuum (Latin *vacuus*, empty), "the world with all the excitations removed."[106] As we get occupied with God (see *vacare Deo* above) we do some emptying and live more simply. Those who are widowed (Latin *viduus*, bereft, without) can speak with authority about having to live with what some might call "a lower degree of symmetry."[107] Simple things like going to the grocery store can take on new meaning—having to choose between paper towels and glancing at oranges absent a loved one may reach new heights for boredom and disgust. Space can become destabilizing. The departure of a loved one, often compelled by unpredictable and uncontrollable circumstances, leaves many things incomplete, and social and psychological adjustments must find a place to locate somewhere between zero and 100. Cultural historian Stephen Kern says that those suddenly placed on empty must establish *de novo* (Latin, again) spatial and cultural distances in order to regain some symmetry. Affairs of the heart can mandate that a person "induce or suppress feeling in order to sustain the outward countenance that produces the proper state of mind in others."[108] The road is long, but the good side can be a growth of the creative process, although at times starting near zero.

There are ways to make empty. We simply sign up for a few weeks of vacation, and sit around unproductively. We know, "[h]olidays make holy; vacations make empty."[109] Empty in Old English was *æmetig*, denoting leisure, interestingly.[110] Iain Gately mentions that blacks decades ago might

31

have felt "less empty" once they were given some alcohol,[111] and Frederick Douglass has remarked that alcohol was "the most effective means in the hands of the slaveholder in keeping down the spirit of insurrection." The alcohol took away a certain emptiness. William James in 1890 has said, "a tract of time empty of experiences seems long in passing, but in retrospect short." Alcohol can alter even the most harmless situations, and empty is heard from again.

Empty can be full, of course, if the discussion is the subjective side of poetry, cornfields, or art. For Mark Doty the "I" of a poem is full, while for Mary Oliver that "I" is empty. The thought reminds us that what seems to be an opposite of something may not so easily be. The same point can be verified by Chicagoans as they go southbound toward Indianapolis by road—the fields of corn along Interstate 65 seem empty and dull to them, but to locals those same fields are full of life, opportunity, and, of course, some profit. Catholics may now be aware of something truly meaningful at a baptism when they renounce Satan "and his empty show," as opposed to a previous wording, "his empty promises." (There *is* something to emptiness in both cases.) Empty was not empty about a hundred years ago to Wassily Kandinsky and Marsden Hartley; for them, emptiness is essential, instructive, and not so vacuous. Newly-constructed hotel lobbies today scream to get filled with the sound of a waterfall or some canned music to conquer the emptiness. In the world of commerce, nothing may seem as empty as a deserted shopping mall, but loud is a different message: there has been some poor planning and a very conscious neglect by potential consumers.

In Catholic theology, none other than the Blessed Virgin Mary gives additional meaning to the term "empty vessel." She so is, although at the same time is filled with the Holy Spirit. She is an *almah* (Hebrew, a young woman), and her role is counter-intuitive, an item probably lost on today's consumer-heavy American culture.[112] She uses her emptiness to serve others. In Ephesians we read of "the fullness of being, the fullness of God himself." Are not some connections obvious here?

Things tend toward zero, and the needle in one's life may not move very much, although we must remember Sergi Avaliani's view: nothing can ever be fully nothing or complete.[113] The scientific community knows that empty (i.e., having matter removed, for now) does not mean that there is no energy present. There indeed is energy, and those located on empty by life's circumstances, whether compelled to be so or not, might use some energy to find a "new normal," wise to believe every step of the way that they are not alone in facing difficulties. Indeed small steps and tiny gains can and do increase. However, an encouragement to get back into the swing of things is pointless: the swing has changed almost beyond recognition. One must work through what Oliver Wendell Holmes, Jr. used to call "the felt necessities of the time." Negative and imaginary numbers were thought by people a few centuries ago to be useless, but now we relate to them easily.

Some people, however, become ghosts, performing oddly. They are "figures," not persons. At what ends up being the final laps of their lives, both Marilyn Monroe and Elvis Presley were on empty, seeking public approval (and money), while being placated in the oddest of ways: with jewelry, applause, and fawning. It is no surprise that athletic coaches beyond measure make two mistakes: they stay too long in their jobs, and they become a mere shadow of themselves. There is no "there" there, and such things also include modern-day athletes who hang on desperately to a past that badly connects to the present, and has a very limited future. (Loss of temporality is part of the recipe for psychosis.) Such people become what John Dupré labels "the furniture of the world."[114] Life becomes a confusing labyrinth (Greek, *laberinthos*, an underground place of twists and turns, with some dead ends). Persons therein always have to be more than what they really are,[115] and cannot "walk the walk." Daniel Dennett adds the word "zombies" to the discussion, and Emmanuel Levinas speaks of "curved space," wherein people are heard by certain others, but maybe not seen that much, or very clearly. The situation may give new meaning to a term that care givers use, "failure to thrive," and death comes to such people one-twelfth of a foot at a time. George Packer says such people spiral downward from being (or having) a persona, a brand, and an empire, and the descent may not be pleasant.

Vacuums in a scientific sense were thought centuries ago not to exist, since vacuums were (or contained) nothing, but that was then; now one knows that vacuums have some energy. Maybe the lesson for today is that one should not glibly say that something (or other) is nothing. Maybe such reasoning was behind the writing of the ad used not long ago by Chubb Insurance: "Who insures you does not really matter. Until it matters." Perhaps like a banshee (Gaelic, *bean sidhe* [or *ben síde*], a female who calls to the spirits of the dead), vacuums not only exist, but play an important role in people's lives; vacuums speak, if one is willing to listen. Samuel Bercholz reminds one and all that empty is not "a crude concept."[116] Grandchildren fill a space in the heart that many parents never knew was empty in the first place. (Nature abhors a vacuum, we know.) Into the space also comes some touching, significant for the person who touches, as well as for the one being touched. The touching takes an ugly twist when people observe some kids being dragged up by their parents, not raised. Emptiness is never just a crude concept, remember.

When one is approaching empty there must be some measuring. Latin tells us that to measure and to "do medicine," mentioned earlier, come from the same root (*mederi*, to heal).[117] Humans must put a number on some uncomfortable things: sadness, grief, sickness, and Stage 4 cancer. Not easy. Oliver Wendell Holmes, Jr. has warned us, "The growth of education is an increase in the knowledge of measure."[118] It is so. The same can be said of spirituality, as it involves a constant need for some calibration (Arabic, *qalib*, a mold for casting). The measuring (Hebrew, *she'ur*) requires that a person be delicate, lest many good deeds and more than a few decent persons become *un*-sung, or *dis*-enchanted. Joseph E. Stiglitz says that if we measure wrong we often do wrong, while Elaine Scarry advises us from a differing angle: pain can "take the measure" of speech. Not least, pain at times cannot be objectified easily, although it can often be immense (from Latin, without measure).

Of little help is the urge to tell people to be perfect, despite the wording in some religious texts to be so. Old-time Catholics have made a perfect act of contrition, and in the gospel of Matthew many have memorized "Be perfect as your heavenly is perfect." *Humanae vitae* in 1968 spoke of "mutual personal perfection" in married couples, and some Canon Law urges a continence that is perfect and perpetual (Latin, *perfectam perpetuamque*, no. 277) on the part of priests (male only, putatively heterosexual, and not necessarily asexual). As if such things were not enough, local Catholic bishops ask at the annual Mass of Chrism to be a "more perfect [*sic*] image of Christ." The awkward wording notwithstanding, those are very tall tasks, and not easy things to measure. Canon Law also mentions a possible basis for the push to perfection; things are established by divine ordinance itself (Latin, *ex ipsa ordinatione divina*, no. 113), and operate, when necessary, by innate right (Latin, *iure nativo*, no. 1254). What else to be, other than perfect, given such an emphasis? By contrast, those who framed the Constitution did so knowing it was not perfect. (The idea made perfect sense!) Setting a deadline for things yields much better results than asking someone to be perfect.

Maybe the important part is to remember what basketball coaches should teach—that practice does *not* make perfect, but it makes [skills] permanent, given a variability in the amount of practice, of course. The ability to dribble a basketball becomes, with hope, permanent in the dribbler, although the activity may not be scientifically or clinically perfect. Michael Jordan was not always perfect at dribbling, and he missed more than half of his shots from two-point range. (Barbara J. King would add that practice makes a rewired brain, but one digresses.) The workings of science tell us repeatedly that being imperfect is the style du jour. Science further informs us that there is a predictable end to things, although assuredly not a perfect end. Are we not becoming socially today perfect strangers to one another? Atheist Robert Green Ingersoll told both theists and atheists decades ago that death provides "only perfect rest."

To return for a moment to mistakes (and we all do), honest mistakes continue to dot the landscape of human life,[119] and much comes down to how we humans deal with those mistakes. English, at least, is full of words that describe things gone a bit awry: sins (theology), errors (baseball), dysfunction (psychology), asymmetry (physics), pathology (medicine), malfunction (technology), etc. The message is clear: things go wrong everywhere, and maybe we must realize throughout, "We see dimly as in a mirror," if not "through a glass darkly" (First Corinthians). Some people are overwhelmed by their own errors; they can be "in pain, covered with aches and bruises."[120] Others take umbrage (Latin, *umbra*, shade) in the face of competition and occasional failing; they run from the heat of the sun.[121] Those who do not confront and integrate the possibility of failing are taking a large risk (Latin, *risicare*, to dare the gods).[122]

All of us encounter a lack of perfection every day, and members of Alcoholics Anonymous remind everyone (in their number!) that alcoholic products, called spirits for good reason, transport a person to a somewhat spiritual, if indeed imperfect, world. That world is one of movement and geography: one chases the good times daily while possibly landing without ceremony on a numbness that targets people of every stripe. Such is the world in which one drink is too many, and 1,000 are not enough. Moving up from some negativity (-10, for example), the addict tries to get to a level place (zero?), but often does not make it, realizing that to drink is to die, and that *not* to drink is also to die. Those addicted would be happy to stop at nothing (or zero) in their recovering, but frequently do not, and often go down and down, to a "low bottom." Some have a drink (or three)

35

to remember what they once were, and more than a few consume a drink (or four) in order to forget who they currently are. The twisted arithmetic shows that a drinking problem is a thinking problem, and since the days of Adam and Eve, more than a few people, once called "inebriates," have seen their lives "spirited away," often while seeking an opposing peace and quiet. Robert Birnberg says that alcohol is "the first truly holistic disease." (He is right.) Consuming large quantities of alcohol may give new meaning to the term "liquid engineering," and a founder of A.A. vividly describes alcoholism as "self-will run riot," a long, long way from any peace and quiet. Alcohol "dissolves resolve," also. Inebriety, an old word, works that way.

Science tells us that in our imperfection there is (a final time) *something* to nothingness. Rollo May has said that anxiety about nothing can become anxiety about something, although there can be what some might call "the gift of desperation." To those on the way up from some negativity, an addictions counselor might suggest, *"Ani hu ha 'Elohim"* (Hebrew, Above all else there is God.) Life is indeed a contest (Greek, *agon*; Arabic, *jihad*), and many days and nights are *"agon*-y." While perfect is not so possible, there is room for some hope—owing to the presence of a higher power, who can take a person out of nothing, so to say. It is noteworthy that we say, "Here goes nothing" before a very difficult task is to be experienced, realizing silently at the time that there is most assuredly something (at risk!) in that nothing. Some people glibly say "It's nothing" to spend $1,000 at the local racetrack, but such an act obviously *is* something. It is often $1,000 lost, gone into thin air. Lawyers may contribute, "An absence of evidence is evidence of absence."

Zero, our recently-arrived friend historically and certainly <u>something</u>, is "[a] symbol of causal necessity,"[123] and numbers "south of zero" are particularly vexing for the mind as well as for the heart.[124] Is not -5 smaller than -3, although it looks larger? Moreover, how does a financial whiz in 2011 say that a deficit of $3 billion cannot be located? Even further, National Football League coach Bud Grant lost four Super Bowls; fellow coach Hank Stram lost but one. Who entered the Hall of Fame first, nine years before the other? Grant, for reasons somewhat mysterious, entered first, though his losing totals in Super Bowls were "more negative" (−4) than that of Stram (−1). Try to show a youngster an absence of two apples (−2) or an oldster the presence of a temperature of −370 on Mercury.[125]

While the desire to accumulate and the tracking of some numbers can unlock some scientific realities (like issues of obvious gravity and needed levity) as well as pedestrian ones (like items of retailing), numbers can wiggle a bit. When numbers are large, many characteristics of people (laziness, jealousy, and envy, e.g.) can nevertheless be hidden from view (like energy is hidden in its mass), but when numbers are small, ironically those items seem to jump out and are noticed by everyone. God can be hidden, too, just like the significance of events whose numbers are daunting, although that significance may be hidden at first view. Mental illness may be easily observable in America's Midlands, say, possibly because there is so little of it, while homeless people in Cleveland, for example, may not be so quickly noticed for the voluminous and rapid comings and goings of the general population there. A number goes beyond itself, so to say: it is one thing to have a class rank of 12 when the class has 250 people in it, and quite another to have that same number when there are only 18 in the group. The numbers must be doing some twisting. (Is this an issue of what is called representation, or diminishing sensitivity?) Is 0.9999 equal to 1? Friendship, whether we have a dozen friends or a thousand, is perhaps not a big thing, but is instead a million small things. At a baseball game when people buy a ticket (a revocable license!), for how many innings are they paying? How is it that temperatures "struggle" to make 70, and later "flirt with" 40? Why does the mind "jiggle" a bit when a person says he will soon give up alcohol forever, but has trouble giving it up for today and tomorrow? Perhaps the mind and the numbers function like the workings of ethnicity and of God—the issue is not truly within an individual, but, more accurately, takes place among individuals.

Fractions in mathematical life are break-ups in real life, and one must learn to live with them. Half a loaf is better than no loaf, and one must own her feelings, especially broken ones. They are often broken and made of today's plastic, not of the steel of yesteryear. The truly difficult part may be to realize that feelings do not legitimate just any kind of behavior: a wronged husband (once labeled Mr. Right, or merely Mr. Right Now) does not have a license to do whatever he wishes. Life is a kludge, "an ill-assorted collection of poorly matching parts, forming a distressing whole," says historian Jackson Granholm.[126] John D. Barrow contributes that the world is "a skein of many strands, knotted and tangled." (Life is not just a lottery, mentioned earlier.) Also, it is not necessarily about finding a person one can live with—the more difficult thing is to find a person one cannot live without. The best way to fight cancer may be to fight it next to a person who has it, in a 1/1 relation. There can be less breakage thereby, and time, with a differing rhythm (Latin, *numerus*), may become more manageable.

Those who say that numbers are slippery have not spoken at length to physics students, who will insist that a number must be firm and precise if an airplane is to take off. Kepler once referred to "all number of things [ ... ] actually finite for the very reason it is a number." Zero, to say a negative word about it, does not help universally in this case; it indicates no direction to the pilots mentioned in the first sentence. Those who receive a grade of Fail on comprehensive exams probably wish they had a number, however flimsy, to tell them by how much they failed. By the way, herein 9.58 is not 10.[127]

Simple adding and subtracting can open our eyes. Verbs, speaking of numbers, have to do with multiplying, while nouns have to do with addition and subtraction. Subtraction, in turn, forces us to expand our conception of how numbers work, claims Steven Strogatz, and Ron Hansen has added that we must learn to subtract (and discard) as we age. Instead of accumulating nouns, so to say, we should *in*-corporate verbs, moving about in order to do well (to make money, to most people) and to do good (read, again, Thérèse or Benedict). Lao Tzu tells us that for knowledge we add, but for wisdom we must subtract. Many, regrettably, do the former without any sense of the latter. We can see, maybe, that intelligence is truly a process, not a thing, and measuring the distance from *dis*-covery to knowledge is critical. The distance is significant.

Some school administrators perform a baffling subtraction each year around the third Thursday of November, reducing to zero the classes 24 hours before that day, arguing that the school is best off *not* to be in session then. In addition (or, by subtraction), they think schools and students are best off *not* to be in session several days preceding said Wednesday, because the week is already shortened and therefore cannot be a typical week. Is a schedule moving toward empty, or zero, educationally better than a more positive one? Why do some draw the line "in reverse" so much?

If life goes from −10 to +10 in its bad moments and in its good across Paul Horwich's "direction of time," how do we put a number on the life of a deceased loved one? By dividing? If the dividend is the person's entire time on this earth, what is the divisor? The result (better, the quotient) is even harder to figure. Do we ascertain an answer by the number of kids a person has raised successfully? Should the dividend be the number of people whom the deceased person loved? Or influenced in a positive way? Should we do some multiplying? Should we *not* look at these things in this way, for the crudeness of the look? This is not a situation described as meaningful or meaningless; it is an issue of encountering what is indeterminate (German, *anschaulishe*). Moreover, for many people in the difficult years life gets worse, often unmanageable. One may need an old spyglass, not a telescope, to do this measuring. These tough, ugly experiences can make either a man or a boy out of a person, or a woman or a girl. Some people crumble, going from being an important name (Spanish, *nombre*) to being an everyday, undistinguished noun (Spanish, *nombre*).

As life and people move along, the number of those who care about us gets smaller and smaller, and missing other people must be further deconstructed, root and branch. In a twist on omissions previously discussed, we miss those gone from our sight, we miss Sunday Mass, and we miss job opportunities. There are all kinds of missings, and there can be both an absence and a presence: the absence of a particular person, and the presence of things that clearly do not take the place of a human person. Few say, "I miss God," the God who is, by the way, "the master of chance and time."[128] Maybe all a person needs is one significant other nearby, albeit one with "a spacious heart" (Hebrew, *rohab leb*), a good heart (Yiddish, *lev tov*), or a pure heart (Arabic, *al-qalb assalim*). John Ford Coley had it right about three decades ago: nights are forever without certain significant people. We are told that God determines who walks into our lives, but we humans decide whom we let walk away, whom we let stay, and whom we refuse to let go. It is not about the good times two people have together; it is about the time the two people have left. The highest number some people may ever need can be two; the two can understand Simone Weil's suggestion that life is not just a matter of asking, "How is it going?" but can instead be an opportunity to inquire more profoundly, "What are you going through?"

## V.

Those who cause their own deaths may know that the action has been over time an option, a sin, a crime, a sickness, and a choice (again). Suicide (or "self-delivery") has survived the years and centuries pretty well (to use an awkward phrase), and it will continue to do so. Maybe those who leave early are unwilling to wait their turn to say goodbye to others, or maybe some depression was just too great. Depression is "the history of an undiscoverable self,"[129] and some never *dis*-cover their very selves. Depression can be like gunshot wounds, self-inflicted, and experts are still studying whether or not the condition can be inherited. Through it all, society tries to remove death from the unpleasant narratives that accompany dying; we try to make death unimaginable. Some lose their lives by taking it, in another awkward phrase, but do not lose their lives in a religious sense—by finding themselves and those around them as Jesus did. The focus may be especially destabilizing at two of the most important times in a person's life—"now and at the hour of our death," while some reject the help of those who try to jump in and rescue. They feel they have no such need.

A number of people may "die from suicide" (an acceptable term) because they cannot sell their own narrative to anyone, including to themselves. There is often a resistance to a change in motion (i.e., inertia). Some go to their graves knowing that they had their own explanations to the very end. To quote economist Gary Becker, it is all about "psychic income," and the investment herein is large, although the return for some may be small. Suicide masks the good things done in a person's life; those who survive should hope that it is the other way around, with life winning out over death. Some say glibly, "It was their time." (It was?) Survivors, in turn, at times paint a picture of ingratitude for the gift of life on the part of those who leave early, although they themselves may have provided no "aid in dying." To deny death and cling to life is wrong, and to deny life and seek death is also wrong. Beneath a suicide there are often very weak social ties that produce a loneliness gone extreme. For the record, pain, at least since 1900, has been Charles Sherrington's phrase, "the psychical adjunct of a protective reflex."

What is dark and what is deep intersect in the negative numbers of depression that lead to "self-determination" (another acceptable term), and the act may be said to be completed, not just committed. Much leads up to the act. While many grieve and fret through difficult days and nights, and as ministers search daily for explanations, survivors must realize two things: their love for the deceased rests on the positive side of zero, and God's love through it all knows no bounds. Such love is unlimited, ∞ to mathematicians. The scene may suggest a Russian saying that the darkness is so filled with something that there is no room for light. What is that something? Is it the something (or nothing) that an addict hopes to fill by continuing with her addiction? It may be best to realize that we are stewards at the end of the day, not owners. We do not "own ourselves." We stand in the darkness, unable at times to dispel it, and we do not own.[130]

A teacher (Sanskrit, *guru*, one who takes people from dark to light) instructs about science and literature and other subjects, but does not teach a person how to respond when one's own death is near. Little wonder that emotional hell can break loose in *all* things (Greek, *pan*, as in pan-ic, pan-acea, and pan-creas [all flesh]). Someone should teach people why society often sequesters the sick and the dying, especially as "all hell" takes place. How to prepare for the end of one's life is not covered in school, and not even in medical school, either. Ivan Illich warned us that we are an "amortal society," wishing to move away from death and its trappings. Things that are transformative, like dying and death, are with some hesitation *dis*-covered or *un*-covered, and probably poorly. Princeton's Jeff Dolven reminds us that there is no center of gravity in these panic-filled situations.

Light, in a differing frame, is truly amazing, whether a particle or a wave. It is beyond time, says Christopher Dewdney, and it is a subtle form of matter. We say light is "like" this or "like" that.[131] St. Augustine spoke of "light which space cannot contain," and, more recently, Monet has said that light dissolves form and softens the focus, giving humans a clarity of physical forms that enables them to make some judgments of value—possibly similar to the workings of grace for theologians. Light "just grows, without direction and without aim,"[132] and maybe it goes out in various directions at differing speeds, for reasons at times unknown. Kind of like praying—at times one does not know where the prayers end up. Kind of like sound waves (in three dimensions) shot from an electric guitar in a garage with the doors wide open. Those who speak Spanish or Italian know that a woman does not just give birth—she gives her baby to light (Spanish, *a luz*; Italian, *alla luce*). We adults must learn to wait until the light changes: at intersections, at sunset, in the observatory, and at times when there is a compelling need for changing behavior and pursuing some spiritual direction. Mathematics, Keith Devlin's "invisible universe," must in this case take a back seat.

Artists in the crowd know that light in the first instance brings with it perspective—we look at everything more intelligently thereby, God included. God said, "Let there be light," not "Let there be water."[133] (We have a conflicted relation to water—God is not said to have created it, but it deals with two God-like items, power and security.) Liturgical musicians in early January sing about "the perfect Light," Jesus, while scientists would argue that light, in a differing style, cannot be perfect.

Night, for its part, is indeed special, since it is so many things. It was "man's fist necessary evil,"[134] and it is also a time when God sings, to hear Léon Bloy tell it. Joseph Stella's *Nocturne*, issued in 1918 maybe, gives the impression that night is something to be entered into, at times at one's peril. Can anyone internalize the work of Vincent van Gogh, "the noble savage of color," and not come away saying that night is not a special place? (Today's artificial light is antithetical to the eternal light of the stars, of course.) Night is referred to myriad times in the music of Andrew Lloyd Webber: "sense it, tremulous and tender."

Those who do not understand the importance of night may have to languish there, especially if they have to work often at that time. It is sociologically for the less privileged. Dreaming must be done between nocturnal shifts, and may be more difficult during the day. For the more privileged, even a glance at the skyline of Hoboken, New Jersey at night, seen from New York, can put ideas of romance in the head. Such thinking is not about making a decision concerning what we will do; it is more about a *very* significant thing, the persons we will become.[135]

Night is a good time to contemplate one's own vulnerability (Latin, *vulnus*, wound). *Vulnus* is neuter, and might be said not to play favorites, guys over gals, or gals over guys. Wounds (and pathogens?) seem to locate themselves in whomever they wish, whenever they wish, however they wish, and wherever they wish, for reasons not always known, although we do know that we encounter God as we become more vulnerable. "A world with no more night," to quote <u>The Phantom</u> again, seems ideal, though pleasantly off the mark. Today's technological frenzy ushers in human vulnerability from the very beginning, but does not speak to it. Also, we increasingly expect a lot from the world of technology, and increasingly very little from each other. There remain loneliness, envy, and greed aplenty, day or night.

At night and at other times our bodies are very important. We adjust our timing to start to sleep, and our body (Latin, *corpus*) follows. The word for body (in Latin) is also neuter, as if to remind both boys and girls that each person, to be sure, both has a body, and less grammatically, "is" one. Further, where we place our body means everything: if we stay home and do the Internet (for work, recreation, and even religion) we may be killing certain institutions, for not moving our bodies out the door. Staying at home makes for empty streets, which makes for empty stores, which makes for financial loss, which makes for mergers and shutdowns, all because of where we choose to locate our bodies, "our first property" according to George Simmel. (Empty again speaks volumes.) Durkheim was right, too: some institutions, like churches, do their best gathering (several) bodies and "in bonding small-scale societies."[136] The hardest part may be philosophical, to realize that we humans are more than just our bodies. Elaine Scarry, again, adds that pain in those bodies makes language more labored.

Stand-up comedians, often working at night, tell jokes about wounding and bodies because they understand that their listeners relate to wounds and vulnerability. Daniel Dennett, certainly not a comedian, adds that our sense of humor has everything to do with hidden and feared things, like aches and pains.[137] The flow of blood (Latin, *sanguis*), too.

Those who are sanguine (and putatively sociable) may know that in the Christian tradition wine becomes blood, even though, lo and behold, the blood looks like wine, tastes like wine, and feels like wine. A life source becomes a spirit, not so different from the product that the local liquor store sells, although the fruit of the vine at a Catholic Mass, fashioned by "the work of human hands," becomes the blood of a wounded man on a wooden cross. Taken away theologically are the sins of those who believe and consume that blood, er, wine. A transformation, or transubstantiation, takes place: substance and accidents, usually thought to be in strict and unchanging alignment, become inverted. The process is significant: one goes from stories to experience, and from believing to feeling. (Historians know that blood and the spirit are mentioned as far back as 1628 by William Harvey.) Those with issues of blood are "an-emic" (from Greek, without blood; better English, insufficient iron). Steve Martin adds that stand-up, which can get bloody, is "the ego's last stand." Blood and blessing are connected etymologically, too: to do stand-up one may bleed a bit, at times with the blessing of the audience. More and more, blood scientifically reveals volumes about human life, one's ethnic background and tobacco habits included. Jennifer Michael Hecht uses the term "entheogen," referring to a substance like wine (converted to blood) that brings with it religious experiences.

Who has not felt a little "God-like" after imbibing a bit, and who has not at a cocktail party blurted out something under the influence, wounding a few people? Remember the Latin *in vino veritas* (in wine [ ... ] truth)? Comedian Tig Notaro, also wounded, jokes about her own Stage 2 breast cancer, and Maria Bamford jokes about her deep and dark side, often to the quiet of her listeners. Audiences can relate to both the deep and the wounds, but often hesitate to laugh or applaud. Pain, of whatever definition, contains messages that each person has to figure out.

To be a bit lighter (and brighter), whether in pain or in a religious mood, a person might wish upon a star. Heaven may indeed be "bright as the stars we're under" (to channel lyricist Dorothy Fields), but uncertainty often wins the day. The light from stars overhead can be thousands of years old, and the gaze is at once backward and, in a dreamy sense, forward. We can get the feeling that we are prolonging our life (in a nice way), as opposed to postponing our eventual death. The stars do move around in the sky (or dome in Genesis), just like human wishing and hoping. Lyricist Sammy Cahn wrote in 1953, "The sky's a blackboard high above you," and he is right: the stars can be white "chalk marks" waiting to be counted, evaluated, and dreamed about. Al McGuire, the late basketball coach at Marquette University, used to say that we humans rush for the stars as we crawl to our graves, a possible twist on the Latin *ad astra per aspera* (to the stars through difficulties). He may have been right, too: ambition can bewilder everyone, even those with 20/20 vision. Verlyn Klinkenborg adds that the lights here on this planet drain the stars of their power. It is not about fleeting romantic things we experience one person to the next. It is not about quick sexual joys, either, and it is not about what we think of ourselves. It is about our ability to gaze, to hope, and to make a plan "beyond ourselves."

Physicists who reference the arrow of time (that is, an egg can become an omelet, but not the other way) are the ones who tell us that we can become wanderers (Greek, *planetes,* as in planets), in part due to errors (from Latin, *errare,* to wander, again), while some become, in a phrase, a traveler (Greek, *ion*) in life. Mounting debt and a messy divorce can cause odd spirals, not circles. Ellipses, like the shape of a football, may better mirror the paths that many lives take. A straight path is seldom the norm, and non-uniform velocities, thanks to the input of Kepler, are to be expected. And just think: there is in all of this some dreaming, and the immensity of space to boot. It may make a person want behaviorally to do some movement (Greek, *kinesis*) and "swing among the stars," to quote Frank Sinatra.

Importantly, zero, an even number by the way, holds things together, but also keeps things apart[138] as the stars swirl. Zero helps the number 2 hang with the number 400 when we write 402. (There was a time when such a thing caused great confusion.) And zero also separates; it keeps –1 away from +1. Separation is not a bad thing: did not God do some separating in Genesis, of light and darkness? And, does God not hold things together, furthermore? Zero reminds some people of language use: things can come together in people's lives, or can move farther apart in a social sense. Languages do both, uniting and separating. Not least, one has to go emotionally through zero in wondering why one person cannot buy one shirt, and why someone else can easily afford a dozen. Holding things together takes place when certain realities come together (Latin, *symbolus*), and the opposite happens when things are scattered (Latin, *diabolus,* also the devil), and humans can become distressed (from Latin, drawn apart). Zero is also versatile; easily it turns (Latin, *versus*), since it is both a number (as in 1+0) and a symbol (as in 10+1), a thought delicious to two groups thought to be different, mathematicians and linguists. Zero in its splendor is co-dependent, we can say.

Mary, the Mother of Jesus and working in the margins, is also the morning star (Latin, *stella matutina*), like Venus, and she and the moon have a long history together as well.[139] Both dress in blue, the color of authority and trustworthiness. (Just ask the local policewoman.) Both are possibly "cool" in McLuhan-esque fashion: Mary and the moon are like the television and the telephone, inviting a deepening participation and involvement on the part of those who commit themselves to them. Further, they converge in the Qu'rán, of all places, where we read two rather important wordings: *ibn maryam*, the son of Mary, and *rasūlu llāh*, the messenger of God. Might there be a case here of occultation? The life of Mary is hidden by the more documented narrative of her son, Jesus, but her small mention is instructive. While many think that Mary is too bland a name today (and was too holy for secular use until the twelfth century), it is nevertheless up to humans to live out her story by modeling her behavior, which, once more, starts with a certain emptying. A simple wording describes what this very important disciple was about: "of Mary was Jesus born."

We have often been enamored of both the moon, with its transience and rebirth, and Mars, but maybe we should not.[140] English majors know that Ray Bradbury has us saying, "Mars is heaven," and he may be right, although Mars and the moon are not so similar.[141] Scientific testing about one does not always give usable results about the other. The moon, for the record, is 400 times smaller than the sun, but the sun ("the national clock") is 400 times farther from the earth than the moon, and through it all we love to reference the moon, a bit heavy at 81 quintillion tons. Mars, meanwhile, had oxygen at one time, and some believe that life on earth could have started on Mars a few billion years ago. The old vaudeville joke is that two men were leaving a bar very early in the morning and could not tell the moon from the sun; one said to the other that he did not know which was which because he did not live in the area.

The water on the moon, or the lack of it, may remind a few that the religious law of Muslim people, *shari'aa* or *shari'a*, means "path to the watering place." It always seems to get back to water, a robust class to scientists for its ability to adapt and change things for better or for worse.[142] Water (Russian, *voda*; into English, vodka) is the incubator of life. Water is like electricity: both travel in a circuit, both move with a little resistance, and both do some resisting themselves. Not unlike people. The *mar* root in many English words (maritime, marine, etc.) means water. Mary, too. Hard to do without it, or her.

Seemingly all humans want the participation of two rather bright objects in the sky, the sun (also called "the lamp of heaven" and a third-generation star) and the moon, mentioned earlier. The sun's heat (passion, possibly) is a good companion to the moon's coolness. (Cool speaks for itself.) The point is that human relations must be at times hands-on, task-centered, and occasionally intense, but also must involve some softer moments, both causing and ending in some serious affect. On December 11, 2117 Venus (aka the Goddess of Love) will cross in front of the sun again, a time of both love and heat. (First reported in 1639, a blocking of the sun, an occultation, also took place on April 24, 1860.) The uncomfortable "dog days" of summer occur when Sirius lines up with *Canis major* (Latin, Greater Dog). Discuss these things with friends who speak French during a party at twilight, *entre le chien et le loup*, between the dog and the wolf, a fleeting time when one cannot easily see the difference between the two. The Hebrew word for evening, *erev*, suggests chaos, as opposed to *boker*, morning, a time of clarity. The Bible recounts a host of things done in the dead of night that are not good. Remember the phrase "darkness all over the land"?

We are warned that the moon (Latin, *luna*) is a harsh mistress, "close enough to touch/But careful if you try," referencing songwriter Jimmy Webb. The danger is that in all loving there can be a letting-go that can discombobulate, harm, and even destroy. (But, the effort always seems worth it.) While part of the moon's job is to induce some dreaming and to soothe, another dimension is one of possession and madness. *Luna*-tics know this turf. The Qu'rān talks of the moon's excessive cold, and indeed it should talk that way, since Islam and the moon have so much to do with one another—it is all about the sighting of a crescent moon. A person would do well to contemplate the workings of the moon away from the lights of a city, indeed out in the boondocks (Tagalog, *bundok*, mountain).

If the question involves the twists of life, and the moon, in order to make decisions, we must do things at the proper time (Greek, *kairos*; Latin, *maturus*). Much of life may be trying to find some pleasant moments located between boredom and disorganization, and mere clock time (Greek, *kronos*) is too simplistic. Time, life's scarcest commodity, is artificial: it is not "a concrete thing lying out there waiting to be parsed out,"[143] and has to it "a puzzling elasticity."[144] A help may be music, which is all about the proper timing; Lejarin Hiller has said that music is "a compromise between monotony and chaos." (Kind of like life.) We are well advised to remember that we are not stressed because we have no time; it is that we have no time because we are stressed. A way to slow down the moving of time may be to learn something (a foreign language or music, e.g.) for the first time. While the Bible tells us in Galatians that things happen in "the fullness of time, we may have to "moonlight" a bit in order to understand all these things. Filipinos know that one word in Tagalog (*buwan*) yields both moon and month.

Time is so elastic (kind of like air) that there is a time for every purpose, the book of Ecclesiastes tells us. There can be a time for this, a time for that, and a time for whatever. When parents are asked about providing a fun activity for their children, they often respond, "There isn't time." In truth, there probably may still be, but other things might come ahead in the planning. Some senior women boast insightfully that they could clean and cook all day years ago, but now it takes them all day to get those things done. Those oldsters may now understand the term "borrowed time."

Is it not imperative that we overturn the feeling that "God is speed and "time is the devil"?[145] Perhaps we should live like Jesus did, with an eye on the future, and the coming kingdom there, while downplaying some momentary pleasures and embracing a few temporary pains. Patience (from Latin, *patior*, a deponent verb having to do with suffering, *not* waiting) will come in handy. It's about time, in a pun.

Life is indeed a fleeting thing, just a jot (from Greek, *iota*). Maybe what works best is a sitting together (Greek, *sanhedrin*) and discussing a desire for some emptiness, the place where this writing first began.

# Endnotes

1. Arnold Herman, *To Think Like God: Pythagoras and Parmenides, the Origins of Philosophy* (Las Vegas, NV: Parmenides Pub., 2004), p. 259. Also, some may enjoy Alberto A. Martínez, *The Cult of Pythagoras: Math and Myths* (Pittsburgh: University of Pittsburgh Press, 2012). In either case, one sees that certain truths are objective, necessary, and timeless.

2. Richard T. Hughes, *Myths America Lives By* (Urbana, IL: University of Illinois Press, 2003). p. 157

3. Philolaus (not Pythagoras) in Vance G. Morgan, *Weaving the World: Simone Weil on Science, Mathematics, and Love* (Notre Dame, IN: University of Notre Dame Press, 2005), p. 71.

4. Hervé Fischer and Rhonda Mullins, *Digital Shock: Confronting the New Reality* (Montreal/Ithaca, NY: McGill-Queen's University Press, 2006), p. 165.

5. The insight comes from Dennis Prager, *Happiness is a Serious Problem: A Human Nature Repair Manual* (New York: ReganBooks, 1999), p. 47.

6. The idea is found in John Cacioppo and William Patrick, *Loneliness* (New York: W. W. Norton & Co., 2008), p. 219.

7. Joseph E. Davis, *Identity and Social Change* (New Brunswick, NJ: Transaction Publishers, 2000), p. 140.

8. James Jordan, *The Musician's Breath: The Role of Breathing in Human Experience* (Chicago: GIA Publications, 2011), pp. 57-62.

9. The wording is a slight paraphrase of Leonard Shlain, *Art & Physics: Parallel Visions in Space, Time, and Light* (New York: Morrow, 1991), p. 188.

10. For more information see Eric Weiner, "God: Some Assembly Required," *Man Seeks God: My Flirtations with the Divine* (New York: Twelve, 2011), pp. 336-340, and "Where Heaven and Earth Come Closer," *New York Times*, Travel, March 11, 2012, p. 10.

11. Marshall McLuhan, *Understanding Media: The Extensions of Man* (New York: New American Library, 1964), p. 348.

12. Michael A. Scaperlanda, "Lawyering in the Little Way of St. Thèrése with Complete Abandonment and Love," *Journal of Catholic Legal Studies*, vol. 46, no. 1 (2007), pp. 43-63.

13. For more, see Charles Seife, *Decoding the Universe: How the New Science of Information is Explaining Everything in the Cosmos, from Our Brains to Black Holes* (New York: Viking, 2006), pp. 8-9. For details on information theory, see Seife's *Proofiness: The Dark Arts of Mathematical Deception or How You're Being Fooled by the Numbers* (New York: Viking, 2010), p. 234.

14. At sidebar, non-depletion can be found in Charles Jonscher, *Evolution of Wired Life: From the Alphabet to the Soul-Catcher Chip—How Information Technologies Change Our World* (New York: Wiley, 1999), p. 176.

15. Concerning crimes of omission, see Michael S. Moore, *Act and Crime: The Philosophy of Action and Its Implications for Criminal Law* (Oxford: Clarendon Press, 1993), pp. 22-34, and for omitting in general, see Myles Brand, "The Language of Not Doing," *American Philosophical Quarterly*, vol. 8, no. 1 (January 1971), pp. 45-53.

16. Sarah Voss, *What Number is God? Metaphors, Metaphysics, Metamathematics, and the Nature of Things* (Albany, NY: State University of New York Press, 1995), p. 124.

17. Eviatar Zerubavel, "Lumping and Splitting: Notes on Social Classification," *Sociological Forum*, vol. 11, no. 3 (1996), pp. 421-433.

18. See David Klinghoffer, *The Discovery of God: Abraham and the Birth of Monotheism* (New York: Doubleday, 2003), p. 298.

19. For "real but without the numbers," see Rollo May, *The Discovery of Being: Writings in Existential Psychology* (New York: Norton, 1983), p. 94.

20. Ray Kurzweil, *The Singularity is Near: When Humans Transcend Biology* (New York: Viking, 2005), p. 2.

21. As a "general" text, see Stephen Cave, *Immortality: The Quest to Live Forever and How It Drives Civilization* (New York: Crown Publishers, 2012).

22. Nicholas Humphry, *Soul Dust: The Magic of Consciousness* (Princeton and Oxford: Princeton University Press, 2011), p. 178.

23. Ellen Ruppel Shell, *Cheap: The High Cost of Discount Culture* (New York: Penguin Press, 2009), p. 57.

24. Wolfgang Schivelbusch, *Disenchanted Night: The Industrialization of Light in the 19$^{th}$ Century* (Berkeley, CA: University of California Press, 1988), p. 178.

25. James Watson, in Leon Jaroff, "Keys to the Kingdom," *Time*, Special Issue, no. 148, no. 14 (Fall 1996), p. 29, and also in Erik Davis, *TechGnosis: Myth, Magic, Mysticism in the Age of Information* (New York: Harmony Books, 1998), p. 130.

26. For some stillness, see Anil Ananthyaswamy, *The Edge of Physics: A Journey to Earth's Extremes to Unlock the Secrets of the Universe* (Boston: Mariner Books, 2011), p. 8. Some may enjoy Ananthyaswamy in "Space against Time," *NewScientist*, vol. 218, no. 2921 (June 15-21, 2013), pp. 35-37.

27. John of the Cross, in E. Allison Peers, trans., *Dark Night of the Soul* (Garden City, NY: Image Books, 1959), p. 157.

28. The phrase is from Jennifer J. Cobb, *Cybergrace: The Search for God in the Digital World* (New York: Crown Publishers, Inc., 1998), p. 167.

29. The intervening (not the interfering) of God is mentioned in James Trefil, *Dark Side of the Universe: A Scientist Explores the Mysteries of the Cosmos* (New York: Scribner's, 1988), pp. 21-22.

30. F. H. Low-Beer, *Questions of Judgment: Determining What's Right* (Amherst, NY: Prometheus Books, 1995), pp. 190-191.

31. Lance Morrow, *Evil: An Investigation* (New York: Basic Books, 2003), p. 37.

32. Greg M. Epstein, *Good Without God: What a Billion Nonreligious People Do Believe* (New York: William Morrow, 2009), pp. 20-21, and Jerry A. Coyne, "You Can Be Good Without God," *USA Today*, August 1, 2011, p. 7A.

33. Krzysztof Burdzy, *The Search for Certainty: On the Clash of Science and Philosophy of Probability* (Hackensack, NJ: World Scientific, 2009), p. 5.

34. Mark Ruwedel, *Dusk*, Haggerty Museum of Art at Marquette University, June 6, 2012-August 5, 2012.

35. Lee C. McIntyre, *Dark Ages: The Case for a Science of Human Behavior* (Cambridge, MA: MIT Press, 2006), p. 95.

36. Stephen L. Carter, *God's Name in Vain: The Wrongs and Rights of Religion in Politics* (New York: Basic Books, 2000), p. 147.

37. James L. Kugel, *In the Valley of the Shadow: On the Foundations of Religious Belief (and Their Connection to a Certain, Fleeting State of Mind)* (New York: Free Press, 2011), p. 149.

38. The house lights in American Catholic churches seem to be brought up to full power less often these days, possibly due to the longstanding decrease of priests, attributable by some to celibacy, in some minds thought on occasion to be "more as a negative than as a positive" (James Martin, SJ, "The Priesthood Today: We Are in This Together," *Catholic Update* [July 2009]), p. 3). Celibacy as a gift to some but made obligatory for all priests is mentioned in James A. Coriden et al., eds., *The Code of Canon Law: A Text and Commentary* (New York/Mahwah, NJ: Paulist Press, 1985), p. 209. The path is clear: "A seminarian of the Latin Church is not going to be called to the priesthood and at the same time not called to celibacy." See Rev. Msgr. Michael Hintz, PhD, "Configured to Christ: Celibacy and Human Formation," in John C. Cavadini, ed., *The Charism of Priestly Celibacy: Biblical, Theological, and Pastoral Reflections* (Notre Dame, IN: Ave Maria Press, 2012), p. 78.

39. The bibliography about fair and unfair is vast. See Paul Woodruff, *The Ajax Dilemma: Justice, Fairness and Rewards* (New York: Oxford University Press, 2011); Michael Schwalbe, *Rigging the Game: How Inequality is Reproduced in Everyday Life* (New York: Oxford University Press, 2008); Nigel Warburton, "Fairness Through Ignorance: John Rawls," in *A Little History of Philosophy* (New York: Yale University Press, 2011), pp. 128-130; Lawrence E. Mitchell, *Stacked Deck: A Story of Selfishness in America* (Philadelphia: Temple University Press, 1998), pp. 94-101; Norman J. Finkel, *Not Fair! The Typology of Commonsense Unfairness* (Washington, DC: American Psychological Association, 2001); Emily R. Gill, "Pass Same-sex on Fairness, Equality Grounds," *Peoria Journal Star*, March 9, 2013, p. A4; and Stephen T. Asma, *Against Fairness* (Chicago and London: University of Chicago Press, 2013).

40. More about wrongs and rights (and deserving) are found in Alan M. Dershowitz, *The Abuse Excuse: And Other Cop-outs, Sob Stories, and Evasions of Responsibility* (Boston: Little, Brown and Company, 1994), pp. 121-124.

41. Richard P. Bentall, *Doctoring the Mind: Is Our Current Treatment of Mental Illness Really Any Good?* (New York: New York University Press, 2009), p. 168.

42. What counts, and what does not, can be seen in Noam Cohen, "When Knowledge Isn't Written, Does It Still Count?" *New York Times*, August 8, 2011, p. B4. New York City, for what it is worth, employs a so-called poverty researcher, a person who counts and measures trends connected with those who do not have.

43. Terry Eagleton, *After Theory* (New York: Basic Books, 2003), p. 178.

44. For a broader discussion on altruism see Robert L. Trivers, "The Evolution of Reciprocal Altruism," *Quarterly Review of Biology*, vol. 46, no. 1 (March 1971), pp. 35-57, as well as his *Folly of Fools: The Logic of Deceit and Self-Deception* (New York: Basic Books, 2011), pp. 77, 81, 281, 309, 313; Philip Kitcher, "The Evolution of Human Altruism," *The Journal of Philosophy*, vol. 90, no. 10 (October 1993), 497-516; Robert Wright, *The Evolution of God* (New York: Back Bay Books, 2010), pp. 25, 80, 473-476, 479-480; and Barbara A. Oakley et al., eds., *Pathological Altruism* (Oxford/New York: Oxford University Press, 2012).

45. For more, see Alina Tugend, *Better By Mistake: The Unexpected Benefits of Being Wrong* (New York: Riverhead Books, 2011), p. 3.

46. The thought comes from Kathryn Schulz, *Being Wrong: Adventures in the Margin of Error* (New York: HarperCollins, 2011), p. 338.

47. Peter Simms, *Little Bets: How Breakthrough Ideas Emerge from Small Discoveries* (New York: Free Press, 2011), p. 53.

48. The insight comes from William A. Miller, *Make Friends with Your Shadow: How to Accept and Use Positively the Negative Side of Your Personality* (Minneapolis: Augsburg Publishing Company, 1981), p. 82.

49. John Polkinghorne, *Theology in the Context of Science* (New Haven: Yale University Press, 2009), p. 117.

50. The idea comes from James P. Carse, *The Silence of God: Meditations on Prayer* (New York Macmillan, 1985), p. 21.

51. Tim Basselin, "Why Theology Needs Disability," *Theology Today*, vol. 68, no. 1 (April 2011), p. 53. In addition, see Burton Cooper, "The Disabled God," *Theology Today*, vol. 49, no. 2 (July 1992), pp. 173-182.

52. Julie Deardorff, "When Weight is Disabling," *Chicago Tribune*, sec. 5, May 1, 2013, pp. 1-2.

53. James C. Howell, *The Will of God: Answering the Hard Questions* (Louisville: Westminster John Knox, 2009), p. 81.

54. For some insight into "pure evil," see Roy F. Baumeister, *Evil: Inside Human Cruelty and Violence* (New York: Henry Holt, 2001), pp. 66-68. A good follow-up might be Terry D. Cooper, *Dimensions of*

*Evil: Contemporary Perspectives* (Minneapolis: Fortress Press, 2007), pp. 196-199.

55. Lisa Appignanesi, *All About Love: Anatomy of an Unruly Emotion* (New York: W. W. Norton & Co., 2011), p. 80.

56. Punishment (not torture!) is found in Jeffrey Reiman, "What is Fair Play?," *Journal of Catholic Social Thought*, vol. 8, no. 1 (Winter 2011), pp. 19-35.

57. The thought comes from sociologist David O. Friedrichs.

58. Concerning punishing, see Sam H. Pillsbury, "The Meaning of Deserved Punishment: An Essay on Choice, Character, and Responsibility," *Indiana Law Journal*, vol. 67, no. 3 (Summer 1992), pp. 719-752; Kenworthey Bilz and John M. Darley, "What's Wrong with Harmless Theories of Punishment?," *Chicago-Kent Law Review*, vol. 79, no. 3 (2004), pp. 1215-1252; and Kevin M. Carlsmith, et al., "Why Do We Punish? Deterrence and Just Deserts as Motives for Punishments," *Journal of Personality and Social Psychology*, vol. 83, no. 2 (August 2002), pp. 285-299. Some may enjoy Andrew Skotnicki, *Religion and the Development of the American Penal System* (Lanham, MD: University Press of America, 2000), and Omar Tonsi Eldakar's work on selfish punishment.

59. The issue can be found in Gary S. Becker, "Crime and Punishment: An Economic Approach," *Journal of Political Economy*, vol. 76, no. 2 (March-April, 1968), pp. 169-217.

60. The thinking comes from Simon May, *Love: A History* (New Haven: Yale University Press, 2011), p. 13.

61. Michael Shermer, *The Believing Brain: From Ghosts and Gods to Politics and Conspiracies—How We Construct Beliefs and Reinforce Them as Truths* (New York: Times Books, 2011), p. 186.

62. Michael Miller in Richard Stivers, *Shades of Loneliness: Pathologies of a Technological Society* (Lanham, MD: Rowman & Littlefield, 2004) p. 56.

63. What Einstein said (in part) can be found in Robert L. Wolke, *What Einstein Told His Barber: More Scientific Answers to Everyday Questions* (New York: Dell Publishing, 2000), p. 100.

64. Cooper, *Sin, Pride, and Self-Acceptance: The Problem of Identity in Theology and Psychology* (Downers Grove, IL: IVP, 2003), p. 122.

65. Corey S. Powell, *God in the Equation* (New York: Free Press, 2002), p. 28.

66. The thought is contributed by Brian Greene, *The Hidden Reality: Parallel Universes and the Deep Laws of the Cosmos* (New York: Alfred A. Knopf, 2011), p. 53.

67. See Luc Ferry, *Man Made God: The Meaning of Life* (Chicago: University of Chicago Press, 2003), p. 85. Ferry refers readers to Simone Weil, *Grace and Gravity* (London/New York: Routledge and Kegan Paul, 1952), p. 1.

68. Herbert Butterfield, *Christianity and History* (London: G. Bell and Sons, Ltd., 1954), p. 39.

69. Geometry has a vast following. See Julian L. Hook, "Hearing with Our Eyes: The Geometry of Tonal Verse," in *Bridges: Mathematical Connections in Art, Music, and Science*, vol. 5 (2002), pp. 123-134; Dmitri Tymoczko, "The Geometry of Musical Chords," *Science*, vol. 313, issue 5783 (July 7, 2006), pp. 72-74; James Franklin, *What Science Knows: And How It Knows It* (New York: Encounter Books, 2009), p. 120; A. Garrett Lisi and James Owen Weatherall, "A Geometric Theory of Everything," *Scientific American*, vol. 303, no. 6 (December 2010), pp. 54-61; Matila C. Ghyka, *The Geometry of Art and Life* (New York: Dover Publications, 1977); Ian Stewart and Martin Golubitsky, *Fearful Symmetry: Is God a Geometer?* (London: Penguin, 1992). Did not Plato call writing "the geometry of the soul"? Some artists may enjoy *Geometric Abstraction* by Abraham Walkowitz, done in 1916. One could add *Hard Edge, Cool Logic: Geometric Abstraction in the 20$^{th}$ Century*, Ft. Wayne Museum of Art, November 2, 2013 – January 26, 2014.

70. Karen Armstrong, *The Case for God* (New York: Alfred A. Knopf, 2009), p. 181.

71. Miranda Lundy, *Sacred Geometry* (New York: Walker & Co., 2001), p. 22.

See also W. D. Hamilton, "Geometry for the Selfish Herd," *Journal of Theoretical Biology*, vol. 31 no. 2 (May 1971), pp. 295-311.

72. For closure's inabilities, see Carie Lemack, "His Death Does Not Bring Me Closure," *USA Today*, May 3, 2011, p. 11A. Paul Pearsall's "openture" may be a better idea.

73. Concerning some memories and their workings, see Laurie Goodstein, "Authors of Church Report on Abuse Defend Their Findings as Critics Weigh In," *New York Times*, May 19, 2011, p. A1.

74. Closure gets a lot of mention. See G. Sulzberger, "As Survivors Dwindle, Tulsa Confronts Past," *New York Times*, May 20, 2011, pp. A16, A18, and about 9/11, see Katharine Q. Seelye, "A Sense of Closure at 9/11 Crash," *New York Times*, September 10, 2011, p. A8.

75. Further, attempts at closure can result in physical changes. See Frank Main and Nicole Weskerna, "It's Not the Same Building," DeKalb (IL) *Daily Chronicle*, January 14-15, 2012, pp. A1, A7, as well as John C. Seitz, *No Closure: Catholic Parishes and Boston's Parish Shutdowns* (Cambridge, MA: Harvard University Press, 2011).

76. Raymond James Teller, in George Johnson, "Sleights of Mind," *New York Times*, August 21, 2007, p. 4. Also, see Rodney Stark, *Discovering God: Origins of the Great Religions and the Evolution of Belief* (New York: HarperOne, 2007).

77. For more details see Naomi Janowitz, *Magic in the Roman World* (London/New York: Routledge, 2001), p. 9, as well as Susan Greenwood, *Anthropology of Magic* (Oxford/New York: Berg, 2009), p. 5.

78. Robert L. Moore and Douglas Gillette, *King, Warrior, Magician, Lover: Rediscovering the Archetypes of the Mature Male* (San Francisco: Harper San Francisco, 1990), p. 107.

79. The point is made by Matthew Hutson, *7 Laws of Magical Thinking: How Irrational Beliefs Keep Us Happy, Healthy, and Sane* (New York: Hudson Street Press, 2012).

80. One would be wise to read the contributions of Cass Sunstein about loss(es) and loss aversion first, and then Bill Hayes, "On Not Being Dead," *New York Times*, November 22, 2012, p. A29.

81. This writing uses zero at almost every turn, but maybe life is a matter of finding the decimal point among the zeroes. Think of a check received as a Christmas bonus. We owe thanks to John Napier for his work on the decimal point in 1614.

82. Douwe Draaisma, *Why Life Speeds Up As You Get Older: How Memory Shapes Our Past* (Cambridge [UK]/New York: Cambridge University Press, 2004), p. 234.

83. Margaret Chizek, RN, "I Can't Remember—Is It Alzheimer's Disease?," Our Lady of Mt. Carmel Church, Darien, IL, November 16, 2011.

84. English majors will recall these words from *Richard II*, Act III, Scene III: "O that I were as great as is my grief, or lesser than my name! Or that I could forget what I have been, Or not remember what I must be now!"

85. Disagreement on the subject is voiced by Matt Ridley in *The Rational Optimist: How Prosperity Evolves* (New York: Harper, 2010), p. 26.

86. Geoffrey Miller, *Spent: Sex, Evolution, and Consumer Behavior* (New York: Viking, 2009), p. 83.

87. Michele Novotni and Randy Petersen, *Angry with God* (Colorado Springs, CO: Piñon Press, 2001), p. 145.

88. One must start somewhere with issues of forgiveness. See David J. Pollay, *The Law of the Garbage Truck: How to Stop People From Dumping on You* (New York: Sterling, 2010), pp. 56-61, and, in a differing way, some may like H. C. J. Godfray, "Animal Behavior: The Evolution of Forgiveness," *Nature*, vol. 355, no. 6357 (January 16, 1992), pp. 206-207.

89. See Jerome Neu, *Sticks and Stones: The Philosophy of Insults* (Oxford/New York: Oxford University Press, 2008), pp. 243-269, and John M. McConnell and David N. Dixon, "Perceived Forgiveness from God and Self-Forgiveness," *Journal of Psychology and Christianity*, vol. 31, no. 1 (Spring 2012), pp. 31-39.

90. For more, see Gerald L. Schroeder, *God According to God: A Physicist Proves We've Been Wrong About God All Along* (New York: HarperOne, 2009). p. 155.

91. Dalton Conley, *The Pecking Order: Which Siblings Succeed and Why* (New York: Pantheon, 2004).

92. Garret Keizer, *The Unwanted Sound of Everything We Want: A Book About Noise* (New York: Public Affairs, 2010), p. 24.

93. Michael Sandel, *Justice: What's the Right Thing to Do?* (New York: Farrar, Straus and Giroux, 2009), p. 142.

94. Gossip gets a nice mention in Matthew Feinberg et al., "The Virtues of Gossip: Reputational Information Sharing as Prosocial Behavior," *Journal of Personality and Social Psychology*, vol. 102, no. 5 (May 2012), pp. 1015-1030; Donna Eder and Janet Lynne Enke, "The Structure of Gossip: Opportunities and Constraints on Collective Expressions among Adolescents," *American Sociological Review*, vol. 56, no. 4, (August 1991), pp. 494-508; and Jeffrey Zaslow, "Before You Gossip, Ask Yourself This...," *Wall Street Journal*, January 16, 2010, pp. B7, B12.

95. David Wolpe, *In Speech and Silence: The Jewish Quest for God* (New York: H. Holt, 1992), p. 191.

96. John Chryssavgis, *In the Heart of the Desert: The Spirituality of the Desert Fathers and Mothers* (Bloomington, IN: World Wisdom, 2003).

97. Timothy K. Beal, *Religion and Its Monsters* (New York: Routledge, 2002), p. 35.

98. George Pattison, *God and Being: An Enquiry* (Oxford/New York: Oxford University Press, 2011), p. 267.

99. For more about things "going right" on Earth, there is John Gribbin, *Alone in the Universe: Why Our Planet is Unique* (Hoboken, NJ: Wiley, 2011).

100. Pierre de Locht, "Death, the Ultimate Form of God's Silence," in Casiano Floristán and Christian Duquoc, eds., *Where is God? A Cry of Human Distress* (London: SCM Press, 1992), pp. 48-56.

101. Hagi Kenaan, *Present Personal: Philosophy and the Hidden Face of Language* (New York: Columbia University Press, 2005), p. 14.

102. Harry M. Collins, *Gravity's Ghost: Scientific Discovery in the Twenty-first Century* (Chicago: University of Chicago Press, 2011), p. 33.

103. Carolyn G. Heilbrun, *Writing a Woman's Life* (New York: Ballantine Books, 1988), p. 21.

104. While the subject of gender is immense, one can start with Warren Farrell, *The Myth of Male Power: Why Men Are the Disposible Sex* (New York: Simon & Schuster, 1993), p. 51; David Brooks, "Why Men Fail," *New York Times*, September 11, 2012, p. A19; and Greg Hampikian, "Men, Who Needs Them?," *New York Times*, August 25, 2012, p. A19. Some may like Stephanie Coontz, "The Myth of Male Decline," *New York Times*, SundayReview, September 30, 2012, pp. 1, 5.

105. The thought is a paraphrase of Heilbrun in *Writing*, p. 95.

106. Anthony Zee, *Fearful Symmetry: The Search for Beauty in Modern Physics* (New York: Macmillan Pub. Co., 1986), p. 219.

107. Joe Rosen, *Symmetry in Science: An Introduction to the General Theory* (New York: Springer-Verlag, 1995), p. 124. Some thoughts about empty are found in Helena Z. Lopata, "Time in Anticipated Future and Events in Memory," *American Behavioral Science*, vol. 29, no. 6 (July–August 1986), pp. 695-709. Greek students know that *eremos* means both desert and empty.

108. Arlie Russell Hochschild, *The Managed Heart: The Commercialization of Human Feeling* (Berkeley, CA: University of California Press, 1983), p. 7.

109. Michael Alec Rose, *Audible Signs: Essays from a Musical Ground* (New York: Continuum, 2010), p. 50, and another source is Karen Stein, "Time Off: The Social Experience of Time on Vacation," *Qualitative Sociology*, vol. 35, no. 3 (September 2012), pp. 335-353.

110. Mark C. Taylor, *Erring: A Postmodern A/theology* (Chicago: University of Chicago Press, 1984). Another feature of empty must

include a mention of Henry Sweet's "empty words," ones that help to hold up a conversation in a subordinate way, to say nothing of Don Ihde and his phenomenology of empty, which is "referential," "directional" and "attentional" in his *Listening and Voice: Phenomenologies of Sound* (Albany, NY: State University of New York Press, 2007), p. 35.

111. The thought is expressed in Iain Gately, *Drink: A Cultural History* (New York: Gotham Books, 2008), p. 311.

112. Todd Tremlin, *Minds and Gods: The Cognitive Foundations of Religion* (New York: Oxford University Press, 2006), pp. 88-89.

113. For those who wish to study zero-point energy, see Paul Halpern, *Edge of the Universe: A Voyage to the Cosmic Horizon and Beyond* (Hoboken, NJ: John Wiley & Sons, 2012), p. 68. See, too, Seife, "The Subtle Pull of Emptiness," *Science*, vol. 275, no. 5297 (January 10, 1997), p. 158, and his *Zero: The Biography of a Dangerous Idea* (New York: Viking, 2000). For a mention of both time and emptiness, see H. Wayne Hogan, "The Perception and Stimulus Preference as a Function of Stimulus Complexity," *Journal of Personality and Social Psychology*, vol. 31, no. 1 (January 1975), pp. 32-35.

114. John Dupré, *Darwin's Legacy: What Evolution Means Today* (Oxford: Oxford University Press, 2003), p. 43.

115. For more, see Hal Niedviecki, *Hello, I'm Special: How Individuality Became the New Conformity* (San Francisco: City Light Books, 2006), p. 10.

116. The phrase "crude concept" is found in Samuel Bercholz and Sherab Chödzin, eds., *Entering the Stream: An Introduction to the Buddha and His Teachings* (Boston: Shambhala, 1993), p. 154, and it can also be seen in Bernard J. Verkamp, *The Sense of Religious Wonder: Epistemological Variations* (Scranton, PA: University of Scranton Press, 2002), p. 81.

117. David Bohm, *Wholeness and the Implicate Order* (London/Boston: Routledge and Kegan Paul, 1980), p. 20.

118. Oliver Wendell Holmes, Jr., "Law in Science and Science in Law," *Harvard Law Review*, vol. 12, no. 7 (February 25, 1898), p. 456.

119. Dershowitz, *The Genesis of Justice: Ten Stories of Biblical Justice That Led to the Ten Commandments and Modern Law* (New York: Warner Books, 2000), p. 97. Some may wish to pursue the "honest and reasonable mistake[s] of fact" herein, while others may find interesting a discussion of God dealing harshly with women (pp. 32-35).

120. Rosabeth Moss Kanter, *Confidence: How Winning Streaks and Losing Streaks Begin and End* (New York: Crown Business, 2004), p. 97.

121. See John Welch, O. Carm., "Failure: Is It Necessary?," *Carmelite Review*, vol. 50, no. 4 (Fall 2011-Winter 2012), p. 22.

122. For more, see Lea Brilmeyer, "Wobble, or the Death of Error," *Southern California Law Review*, vol. 59, no. 2 (January 1986), pp. 363-389.

123. Otto Spengler in Sal Restivo, *The Social Relations of Physics, Mysticism, and Mathematics: Studies in Social Structure, Interests, and Ideas* (Dordrecht, Holland and Boston: Kluwer Academic Publishers, 1983), p. 213.

124. Brian Butterworth, *What Counts: How Every Brain is Hardwired for Math* (New York: Free Press, 1999), pp. 322-323.

125. Some linguists know of zero-syllables. People say "wooden" when others might hear "wood." A zero-syllable is at the end of "wooden." It is a W, an unstressed (read: weak) syllable. See Roger Lass, *The Shape of English: Structure and History* (London: Dent, 1987), pp. 108-109. Further, fans of Daniel Dennett will mention his use of zero-order intentionality, and admirers of Sol Steinmetz will remember his zero derivation words, those that derive without a change of form. And to think we have not yet discussed James R. Hurford's zero-place predicates, as in "It's hot," found in his *Origins of Meaning: Language in the Light of Evolution* (Oxford/New York: Oxford University Press, 2007), p. 89.

126. Jackson Granholm in David J. Linden, *The Accidental Mind: How Brain Evolution Has Given Us Love, Memory, Dreams, and God* (Cambridge, MA: Belknap Press of Harvard University Press, 2007), p. 6. Further, Steven M. Teles, for his part, tells us that a kludge is a poorly designed software patch intended to solve an immediate problem.

127. Charles Jonscher, *The Evolution of Wired Life: From the Alphabet to the Soul-catcher Chip—How Information Technologies Change Our World* (New York: Wiley, 1999), p. 49.

128. Kenneth R. Miller, *Finding Darwin's God: A Scientist's Search for Common Ground Between God and Evolution* (New York: Cliff Street Books, 1999), pp. 242-243.

129. Alain Ehrenberg, *The Weariness of the Self: Diagnosing the History of Depression in the Contemporary Age* (Montreal/Ithaca, NY: McGill-Queens University Press, 2010), p. 11.

130. Concerning the workings of grief, see Herbert Hendin, *Suicide in America* (New York: Norton, 1982) and Ruth Davis Konigsberg, *The Truth About Grief: The Myth of Its Five Stages and the New Science of Loss* (New York: Simon & Schuster, 2011), pp. 95-97.

131. A. G. Cairns-Smith, *Secrets of the Mind: A Tale of Discovery and Mistaken Identity* (New York: Copernicus, 1999), p. 173.

132. Evelyn Fox Keller, *Secrets of Life, Secrets of Death: Essays on Language, Gender, and Science* (New York: Routledge, 1992), p. 81.

133. The insight is from Schlain, *Art & Physics*, p. 79.

134. A. Roger Ekirch, *At Day's Close: Night in Times Past* (New York: Norton, 2005), p. 3.

135. Russ B. Connors, Jr., and Patrick T. McCormick, *Character, Choices & Community: Three Faces of Christian Ethics* (New York/Mahwah, NJ: Paulist Press, 1998), p. 38.

136. R.I.M. Dunbar, *How Many Friends Does One Person Need: Dunbar's Number and Other Evolutionary Quirks* (Cambridge, MA: Harvard University Press, 2010), p. 291. Linguists know that "synagogue" can be a synonym for people coming together.

137. Daniel C. Dennett, *Breaking the Spell: Religion as a Natural Phenomenon* (New York: Viking, 2006), p. 53.

138. Robert Kaplan, *The Nothing That Is: A Natural History of Zero* (Oxford/New York: Oxford University Press, 2000), p. 194.

139. James Attlee, *Nocturne: A Journey in Search of Moonlight* (Chicago: University of Chicago, 2011), pp. 46, 49, 55, 91, 93.

140. For more on the relation, see Robert Zubrin and Richard Wagner, *The Case for Mars: The Plan to Settle the Red Planet and Why We Must* (New York: Free Press, 1996), p. 149.

141. John Gribbin, *Alone in the Universe: Why Our Planet is Unique* (Hoboken, NJ: Wiley, 2011).

142. Several photographers contributed to *Dark Blue: The Water as Protagonist*, Haggerty Museum of Art at Marquette University, January 16 – May 19, 2013.

143. Anthony F. Aveni, *Empires of Time: Calendars, Clocks, and Cultures* (New York: Basic Books, 1989), p. 64.

144. Michael G. Flaherty, *Watched Pot: How We Experience Time* (New York: New York University Press, 1999), p. 26.

145. John Thackara, *In the Bubble: Designing in a Complex World* (Cambridge, MA: MIT Press, 2005), pp. 29-33. The reference is to Hitachi's portable computer division, in Mary Jane Ryan, *The Power of Patience: How to Slow the Rush and Enjoy More Happiness, Success, and Peace of Mind Every Day* (Manchester, VT: Northshire, 2003).

# Additional Reading

Aaron, Rabbi David. *The Secret Life of God: Discovering the Divine Within You* (Boston: Shambhala Publications, 2004).

Adams, Scott. *God's Debris: A Thought Experiment* (Kansas City, MO: Andrews McMeel, 2001).

Alexander, Eben, MD. *Proof of Heaven: A Neurosurgeon's Journey into the Afterlife* (New York: Simon & Schuster Paperbacks, 2012).

Alper, Matthew. *The 'God' Part of the Brain: A Scientific Interpretation of Human Spirituality and God* (Naperville, IL: Sourcebooks, Inc., 2006).

Alston, William. *Perceiving God: The Epistemology of Religious Experience* Ithaca, NY: Cornell University Press, 1991).

Altman, Gerry T.M. *The Ascent of Babel: An Exploration of Language, Mind, and Understanding* (Oxford: Oxford University Press, 1997).

Anderson, Pamela Sue. "Can We Love as God Loves?," *Theology & Sexuality*, vol. 12, no. 2 (January 2006), pp. 143-164.

Armstrong, Karen. *A History of God: The 4000-year Quest of Judaism, Christianity, and Islam* (New York: Alfred A. Knopf: Distributed by Random House, 1993).

Assante, Julia, MD. *The Last Frontier: Exploring the Afterlife and Transforming Our Fear of Death* (Novato, CA: New World Library, 2012).

Aveni, Anthony F. *Uncommon Sense: Understanding Nature's Truths Across Time and Culture* (Boulder, CO: University Press of Colorado, 2006).

Axelrod, Robert, and William D. Hamilton. "The Evolution of Cooperation," *Science*, vol. 211, no. 4489 (March 27, 1981), pp. 1390-1396.

Baker, Joseph O. "An Investigation of the Sociological Patterns of Prayer Frequency and Content," *Sociology of Religion*, vol. 69, no. 2 (Summer 2008), pp. 169-185.

Barash, David P. *Homo Mysterious: Evolutionary Puzzles of Human Nature* (New York: Oxford University Press, 2012).

Barber, Nigel. *Kindness in a Cruel World: The Evolution of Altruism* (Amherst, NY: Prometheus Books, 2004).

Barbour, Ian G. *When Science Meets Religion* (San Francisco: HarperSanFrancisco, 2000).

Barr, Stephen M. *Modern Physics and Ancient Faith* (Notre Dame, IN: University of Notre Dame Press, 2003).

Barrett, Justin L. *Why Would Anyone Believe in God?* (Walnut Creek, CA: AltaMira Press, 2004).

Barrow, John D. *Pi in the Sky: Counting, Thinking, and Being* (Oxford, England: Clarendon Press, 1992).

_____. *New Theories of Everything: The Quest for Ultimate Explanation* (Oxford/New York: Oxford University Press, 2007).

Barry, William A. "How Do I Know It's God?," *America*, vol. 186, no. 17, (May 20, 2002), pp. 12-15.

Batson, C. Daniel, and Laura L. Shaw. "Evidence for Altruism: Toward a Pluralism of Prosocial Motives," *Psychological Inquiry*, vol. 2, no. 2 (1991), pp. 107-122.

Battin, Margaret Pabst. *The Least Worst Death: Essays in Bioethics on the End of Life* (New York: Oxford University Press, 1994).

Bennett, Charles H. "Demons, Engines and the Second Law," *Scientific American*, vol. 257, no. 5 (November 1987), pp. 108-116.

Benson, Herbert, et al. "Study of the Therapeutic Effects of Intercessory Prayer (STEP) in Cardiac Bypass Patients: A Multicenter Randomized Trial of Uncertainty and Certainty of Receiving Intercessory Prayer," *American Heart Journal*, vol. 151, no. 4 (April 4, 2006), pp. 934-942.

Berenson, Michael A. "The Wrongful Life Claim—The Legal Dilemma of Existence Versus Nonexistence: 'To Be or Not to Be'," *Tulane Law Review*, 64, no. 4 (March 1990), pp. 895-918.

Bergen, Benjamin K. *Louder Than Words: The New Science of How the Mind Makes Meaning* (New York: Basic Books, 2012).

Berlinski, David. *The Devil's Delusion: Atheism and Its Scientific Pretensions* (New York: Crown Forum, 2008).

Berns, Nancy. *Closure: The Rush to End Grief and What It Costs Us* (Philadelphia: Temple University Press, 2011).

Bickerton, Derek. *Adam's Tongue: How Humans Made Language, How Language Made Humans* (New York: Hill and Wang, 2009).

Black, Don. *Moral Time* (New York: Oxford University Press, 2011).

Bleimaier, John Kuhn. "God, Man and the Law," *Catholic Lawyer*, vol. 39, no. 4 (Winter 2000), pp. 277-290.

Bloom, Howard K. *The God Problem: How a Godless Cosmos Creates* (Amherst, NY: Prometheus Books, 2014).

Bloom, Paul. *Just Babies: The Origins of Good and Evil* (New York: Crown Publishers, 2013).

Bogaert, Anthony F. *Understanding Asexuality* (Lanham, MD: Rowman & Littlefield Publishers, 2012).

Bojowald, Martin. *Once Before Time: A Whole Story of the Universe* (New York: Alfred A. Knopf, 2010).

Bonanno, George A. *The Other Side of Sadness: What the New Science of Bereavement Tells Us about Life After Loss* (New York: Basic Books, 2009).

Borg, Marcus J., and Ross Mackenzie. *God at 2000* (Harrisburg, PA: Morehouse Publishing, 2000).

Bower, Joe. "The Dark Side of Light," *Audubon*, vol. 102, no. 2 (March–April, 2000), pp. 92-97.

Bowker, John. *The Meanings of Death* (Cambridge/New York: Cambridge University Press, 1991).

———. *God: A Brief History* (London/New York: DK Publishing, Inc., 2002).

Boyd, Gregory A. *Is God to Blame? Beyond Pat Answers to the Problem of Suffering* (Downers Grove, IL: InterVarsity Press, 2003).

Boyer, Pascal. *Religion Explained: The Evolutionary Origin of Religious Thought* (New York: Basic Books, 2001).

Brockman, John. *What We Believe But Cannot Prove: Today's Leading Thinkers on Science in the Age of Certainty* (New York: Harper Perennial, 2006).

Brown, Brené. *The Gifts of Imperfection: Letting Go of Who You Think You Are Supposed to Be and Embracing Who You Are* (Center City, MN: Hazelden, 2010).

Brown, Erica. *Happier Endings: Overcoming the Fear of Death: A Mediation on Life and Death* (New York: Simon and Schuster, 2013).

Buenting, Joel. *The Problem of Hell: A Philosophical Anthology* (Burlington, VT: Ashgate Publishing Co., 2010).

Burkeman, Oliver. *The Antidote: Happiness for People Who Can't Stand Positive Thinking* (New York: Faber and Faber, 2012).

Buss, David M. "The Evolution of Happiness," *American Psychologist*, vol. 55, no. 1 (January 2000), pp. 15-23.

Butler, Katy. *Knocking on Heaven's Door: The Path to a Better Way of Death* (New York: Scribner, 2013).

Cairns-Smith, A. G. *Secrets of the Mind: A Time of Discovery and Identity* (New York: Springer-Verlag, Inc., 1999).

Campbell, Jeremy. *Grammatical Man: Information, Entropy, Language, and Life* (New York: Simon and Schuster, 1982).

Capon, Robert Farrar. *Fingerprints of God: Tracking the Divine through a History of Images* (Grand Rapids, MI/Cambridge [UK]: Wm. B. Eerdmans Publishing Company, 2000).

Carse, James P. *The Silence of God: Meditations on Prayer* (San Francisco: HarperSanFrancisco, 1995).

Casey, Michael. *Toward God: The Ancient Wisdom of Western Prayer* (Ligouri, MO: Triumph Books, 1996).

Cashford, Jules. *The Moon: Myth and Image* (New York: Four Walls Eight Windows, 2003).

Casti, John L. *Paradigms Regained: A Further Exploration of the Mysteries of Modern Science* (New York: HarperCollins, 2000).

Cave, Stephen. *Immortality: The Quest to Live Forever and How It Drives Civilization* (New York: Crown Publishers, 2011).

Cervero, Fernando. *Understanding Pain: Exploring the Perception of Pain* (Cambridge, MA and London: The MIT Press, 2012).

Charry, Ellen T. "God and the Art of Happiness," *Theology Today*, vol. 68, no. 3 (October 2011), pp. 238-252.

Chittester, Joan. *The Monastery of the Heart: An Invitation to a Meaningful Life* (Katonah, NY: BlueBridge, 2011).

Chryssavgis, John. *Light through Darkness* (Maryknoll, NY: Orbis Books, 2004).

Clark, Andy. *Being There: Putting Brain, Body and World Together Again* (Cambridge, MA: MIT, 1997).

Clegg, Brian. *The God Effect: Quantum Entanglement, Science's Strangest Phenomenon* (New York: St. Martin's Press, 2006).

_____. *Gravity: How the Weakest Force in the Universe Shaped Our Lives* (New York: St. Martin's Press, 2012).

Cobb, Jennifer J. *CyberGrace: The Search for God in the Digital World* (New York: Crown Publishing, Inc., 1998).

Coffey, Kathy. *God in the Moment: Making Every Day a Prayer* (Chicago: Loyola Press, 1999).

Cohen, Patricia. *In Our Prime: The Invention of Middle Age* (New York: Scribner, 2012).

Cohen, Richard. *Chasing the Sun: The Epic Story of the Star That Gives Us Life* (New York: Random House, 2010).

Collins, Francis S. *The Language of God: A Scientist Presents Evidence for Belief* (New York: Free Press, 2006).

Consolmano, Guy. *God's Mechanics: How Scientists and Engineers Make Sense of Religion* (San Francisco: Jossey-Bass, 2008).

Cooper, Burton Z. *Why, God?* (Atlanta: John Knox Press, 1988).

Corballis, Michael C. *The Recursive Mind: The Origins of Human Language, Thought, and Civilization* (Princeton, NJ: Princeton University Press, 2011).

Corey, Michael A. *The God Hypothesis: Discovering Design in Our 'Just Right' Universe* (Lanham, MD: Rowman & Littlefield, 2001).

Cote, Richard G., OMI. "God Sings in the Night: Ambiguity as an Invitation to Believe," in Christian Duquoc and Casiano Floristán, eds., *Where is God? A Cry of Human Distress* (London: SCM Press, 1992), pp. 95-105.

Coutinho, Paul, SJ. *How Big is Your God? The Freedom to Experience the Divine* (Chicago: Loyola Press, 2007).

Cox, Brian. *The Quantum Universe (And Why Anything That Can Happen, Does)* (Boston: DaCapo Press, 2012).

_____, and Jeff Forshaw. *Why Does $E=mc^2$? And Why Should We Care?* (Cambridge, MA: DaCapo Press, 2009).

Coyne, George V., and Michael Heller. *A Comprehensive Universe: The Interplay of Science and Theology* (New York: Springer, 2008).

Craig, William Lane. "God and Real Time," *Religious Studies*, vol. 26, no. 3 (September 1990), pp. 335-347.

Cray, Dan. "God vs. Science," *Time.com*, November 5, 2006, *www.time.com/time/magazine/article/0,9171,1555132-3,00.html* (accessed July 17, 2012).

Crease, Robert P. *World in the Balance: The Quest for an Absolute System of Measurement* (New York: W.W. Norton, 2011).

Crick, Francis. *What Mad Pursuit: A Personal View of Scientific Discovery* (New York: Basic Books, 1988).

Cusick, Michael John. *Surfing for God: Discovering the Divine Desire Beneath Sexual Struggle* (Nashville: Thomas Nelson, 2012).

Cyrulnik, Boris. *The Whispering of Ghosts: Trauma and Resilience* (New York: Other Press, 2005).

Daalen, Lydia Kim-van. "The Holy Spirit, Common Grace, and Secular Psychotherapy," *Journal of Psychology and Theology*, vol. 40, no. 3 (Fall 2012), pp. 229-239.

Dantzig, Tobias. *Number, The Language of Science: A Critical Survey Written for the Cultured Non-Mathematician* (New York: Pi Press, 2005).

Davies, P. C. W. *God and the New Physics* (New York: Simon & Schuster, 1983).

DeBotton, Alain. *Religion for Atheists: A Non-Believers Guide to the Uses of Religion* (New York: Pantheon Books, 2012).

Dehaene, Stanislaus. *The Number Sense: How the Mind Creates Math* (New York: Oxford University Press, 1997).

Deutsch, David. *The Beginning of Infinity: Explanations That Transform the World* (New York: Viking, 2011).

Deutsher, Guy. *Through the Language Glass: Why the World Looks Different in Other Languages* (New York: Metropolitan Books/Henry Holt and Co., 2010).

Devlin, Keith. *The Math Gene: How Mathematical Thinking Evolved and Why Numbers are Like Gossip* (New York: Basic Books, 2000).

Dewdney, Christopher. *Soul of the World: Unlocking the Secrets of Time* (Toronto: HarperCollins, 2008).

Dickerson, Matthew. *The Mind and the Machine: What It Means to Be Human and Why It Matters* (Grand Rapids: Brazos Press, 2011).

Dossey, Larry. *Recovering the Soul: A Scientific and Spiritual Approach* (New York: Bantam Books, 1989).

Douthat, Ross. *Bad Religion: How We Became a Nation of Heretics* (New York: Free Press, 2012).

Dowd, Maureen. "Why, God?," *New York Times*, December 26, 2012, p. A19.

Dubos, René J. *A God Within* (New York: Scribner, 1972).

Edis, Taner. *The Ghost in the Universe* (Amherst, NY: Prometheus Books, 2002).

Ehrman, Bart D. *God's Problem: How The Bible Fails to Answer Our Most Important Question—Why We Suffer* (New York: HarperOne, 2008).

Einolf, Christopher J. "The Link Between Religion and Helping Others: The Role of Values, Ideas, and Language," *Sociology of Religion*, vol. 72, no. 4 (Winter 2011), pp. 435-455.

Eire, Carlos M. N. *A Very Brief History of Eternity* (Princeton, NJ: Princeton University Press, 2010).

Elwes, Richard. *Mathematics without the Boring Bits: Get a Grip on Infinity, Irrational Numbers, Chaos Theory, and Much More* (New York: Metro Books, 2011).

Epstein, Mark. *The Trauma of Everyday Life* (New York: The Penguin Press, 2013).

Fagg, Lawrence W. *The Becoming of Time: Integrating Physical and Religious Time* (Atlanta: Scholars Press, 1995).

Falk, Dan. *In Search of Time: The History, Physics, and Philosophy of Time* (New York: Thomas Dunne Books/St. Martin's Griffin, 2008).

Farrington, Debra K. *Hearing with the Heart: A Gentle Guide for Discerning God's Will for Your Life* (San Francisco: Jossey-Bass, 2003).

Fehr, Ernst, and Urs Fischbacher. "The Nature of Human Altruism," *Nature*, vol. 425, issue 6960 (October 23, 2003), pp. 785-791.

_____, and Klaus M. Schmidt. "A Theory of Fairness, Competition, and Cooperation," *Quarterly Journal of Economics*, vol. 114, issue 3, (August 1999), pp. 817-868.

Feinberg, Joel. *Doing and Deserving: Essays in the Theory of Responsibility* (Princeton, NJ: Princeton University Press, 1970).

Ferguson, Kitty. *The Fire in the Equations: Science, Religion, and the Search for God* (Philadelphia: Templeton Foundation Press, 2004).

Firestein, Stuart. *Ignorance: How It Drives Science* (New York: Oxford University Press, 2012).

Flaherty, Michael G. *The Textures of Time: Agency and Temporal Experience* (Philadelphia: Temple University Press, 2011).

Flood, Gavin D. *The Ascetic Self: Subjectivity, Memory, and Tradition* (Cambridge/ New York: Cambridge University Press, 2004).

Foley, Duncan K. *Adam's Fallacy: A Guide to Economic Theology* (Cambridge, MA: Belknap Press of Harvard University, 2006).

Foutz, Thomas Keasler. "'Wrongful Life': The Right Not to Be Born," *Tulane Law Review*, vol. 54, no. 2 (February 1980), pp. 480-499.

Foy, George F. *Zero Decibels: The Quest for Absolute Silence* (New York: Scribner, 2010).

Frank, Adam. *About Time: Cosmology and Culture at the Twilight of the Big Bang* (New York: Free Press, 2011).

Fredrickson, Barbara L. *Love 2.0: How Our Supreme Emotion Affects Everything We Feel, Think, Do, and Become* (New York: Hudson Street Press, 2013).

Fuller, Robert C. *Wonder: From Emotion to Spirituality* (Chapel Hill, NC: University of North Carolina Press, 2006).

———. *The Body of Faith: A Biological History of Religion in America* (Chicago: University of Chicago Press, 2013).

Galison, Peter. "Einstein's Clock: The Place of Time," *Critical Inquiry*, vol. 26, no. 2 (Winter 2000), pp. 355-389.

Garfield, Jay L. *Empty Words: Buddhist Philosophy and Cross-cultural Interpretation* (New York: Oxford University Press, 2002).

Garrow, David J. "The Right to Die: Death with Dignity in America," *Mississippi Law Journal*, vol. 68, no. 2 (Winter 1988), pp. 407-430.

Gazalé, Midhat J. *Number: From Ahmes to Cantor* (Princeton, NJ: Princeton University Press, 2000).

Gazzaniga, Michael. *Human: The Science Behind What Makes Us Unique* (New York: Ecco, 2008).

Gingerich, Owen. *God's Universe* (Cambridge, MA: Belknap Press of Harvard University Press, 2006).

Gleick, James. *The Information: A History, A Theory, A Flood* (New York: Pantheon Books, 2011).

Glenberg, Arthur M. "What Memory Is For," *Behavioral and Brain Sciences*, vol. 20, no. 1 (March 1997), pp. 1-55.

Goldberg, Carl. *The Evil We Do: The Psychoanalysis of Destructive People* (Amherst, NY: Prometheus Books, 2000).

Goldberg, Steven. *Seduced by Science: How American Religion Has Lost Its Way* (New York: New York University Press, 1999).

Goldsmith, Mike. *Discord: The Story of Noise* (Oxford: Oxford University Press, 2012).

Gordon, Richard. *The Alarming History of Medicine* (New York: St. Martin's Press, 1994).

Graham, Loren, and Jean-Michel Kantor. *Naming Infinity: A True Story of Religious Mysticism and Mathematical Creativity* (Cambridge, MA: Belknap Press of Harvard University Press, 2009).

Gray, Kurt, and Daniel M. Wegner. "Blaming God for Our Pain: Human Suffering and the Divine Mind," *Personality and Social Psychology Review*, vol. 14, no. 1 (February 2010), pp. 7-16.

Greene, Brian. *Elegant Universe: Superstrings, Hidden Dimensions, and the Quest for the Ultimate Theory* (New York: Vintage Books, 2000).

Greenfield, Kent. *The Myth of Choice: Personal Responsibility in a World of Limits* (New Haven, CT: Yale University Press, 2011).

Groopman, Jerome. "God at the Bedside," *New England Journal of Medicine*, vol. 350, no. 12 (March 18, 2004), pp. 1176-1178.

Gubar, Susan. "With Cancer, a Different Rhythm to Life," *New York Times*, November 20, 2012, p. D6.

Haack, Susan. *Defending Science—Within Reason: Between Scientism and Cynicism* (Amherst, NY: Prometheus Books, 2003).

Haase, Albert, OFM. *Coming Home to Your True Self: Leaving the Emptiness of False Attractions* (Downers Grove, IL: IVP Books, 2008).

Hagerty, Barbara Bradley. *Fingerprints of God: The Search for the Science of Spirituality* (New York: Riverhead Books, 2009).

Haisch, Bernard. *The God Theory: Universes, Zero-point Fields and What's Behind It All* (San Francisco: WeiserBooks, 2006).

Halifax, Joan. *Being with Dying: Cultivating Compassion and Fearlessness in the Presence of Death* (Boston: Shambhala, 2008).

Hamer, Dean H. *The God Gene: How Faith is Hardwired into Our Genes* (New York: Doubleday, 2004).

Hamm, Dennis, SJ. "Rummaging for God: Praying Backward Through Your Day," *America*, vol. 170, no. 17 (May 14, 1994), pp. 22-23.

Hammond, Claudia. *Time Warped: Unlocking the Mysteries of Time* (Toronto: Anansi International, 2012).

Hardcastle, Valerie Gray. *The Myth of Pain* (Cambridge, MA/ London: The MIT Press, 1999).

Harrison, Marissa A., and Jennifer C. Shortall. "Women and Men in Love: Who Really Feels It and Says It First?," *Journal of Social Psychology*, vol. 151, no. 6 (November-December, 2011), pp. 727-736.

Hart, William. *Evil: A Primer: A History of a Bad Idea from Beelzebul to Bin Laden* (New York: Thomas Dunne Books, 2004).

Haught, John F. *Making Sense of Evolution: Darwin, God, and the Drama of Life* (Louisville: Westminster John Knox Press, 2010).

Hecht, Jennifer Michael. *Stay: A History of Suicide and the Philosophies Against It* (New Haven, CT: Yale University Press, 2014).

Heft, James L., et al. *Learned Ignorance: Intellectual Humility Among Jews, Christians, and Muslims* (Oxford: Oxford University Press, 2011).

Henry, Patrick. *The Ironic Christian's Companion: Finding the Marks of God's Grace in the World* (New York: Riverhead Books, 1999).

Hersh, Reuben, and Vera John-Steiner. *Loving + Hating Mathematics* (Princeton, NJ: Princeton University Press, 2011).

Heschel, Abraham Joshua. *God in Search of Man: A Philosophy of Judaism* (New York: Farrar, Straus & Cudahy, 1955).

Higgins, E. Tory. "Beyond Pleasure and Pain," *American Psychologist*, vol. 52, no. 12 (December 1997), pp. 1280-1300.

Hincks, Adam D. "Wonders of the Universe," *America*, vol. 206, no. 13 (April 16-23, 2012), pp. 11-14.

Hitchens, Christopher. *Mortality* (New York: Twelve, 2012).

Hitchings, Henry. *The Secret Life of Words: How English Became English* (New York: Farrar, Straus and Giroux, 2008).

Hopkins, Keith. *A World Full of Gods: The Strange Triumph of Christianity* (New York: Free Press, 2000).

Horgan, John. *Rational Mysticism: Dispatches From the Border Between Science and Spirituality* (Boston: Houghton Mifflin, 2003).

Horowitz, Seth S. *The Universal Sense: How Hearing Shapes the Mind* (New York: Bloomsbury, 2012).

Howard, Deborah. *Where is God in All of This? Finding God's Purpose in Our Suffering* (Phillipsburg, NJ: P & R Pub., 2009).

Humez, Alexander, and Nicholas D. Humez. *On the Dot: The Speck That Changed the World* (New York: Oxford University Press, 2008).

Humphry, Derek and Ann Wickett. *Right to Die: Understanding Euthanasia* (New York: Harpercollins, 1986).

Humphry, Nicholas. *Soul Dust: The Magic of Consciousness* (Princeton, NJ: Princeton University Press, 2011).

Hyde, Michael J. *Perfection: Coming to Terms with Being Human* (Waco, TX: Baylor University Press, 2010).

Ifrah, Georges, and David Bellos. *The Universal History of Numbers: From Prehistory to the Invention of the Computer* (New York: Wiley, 2000).

Impey, Chris. *How It Ends: From You to the Universe* (New York: W. W. Norton, 2010).

Jamison, Kay Redfield. *Night Falls Fast: Understanding Suicide* (New York: Vintage Books, 2000).

Johnson, Dominic D. P., and Oliver Krüger. "The Good of Wrath: Supernatural Punishment and the Evolution of Cooperation," *Political Theology*, vol. 5, no. 2 (April 2004), pp. 159-176.

Johnson, George. "Deep in Universe's Software Lurk Beautiful, Mysterious Numbers," *New York Times*, May 20, 2003, p. D3.

Jones, Dennis Merritt. *The Art of Uncertainty: How to Live in the Mystery of Life and Love It* (New York: Jeremy P. Tarcher/Penguin, 2011).

Jonscher, Charles. *The Evolution of Wired Life: From the Alphabet to the Soul-Catcher Chip—How Information Technologies Change Our World* (New York: Wiley, 1999).

Kadish, Sanford H. "Letting Patients Die: Legal and Moral Reflections," *California Law Review*, vol. 80, no. 4 (July 1992), pp. 857-888.

Kagan, Jerome. *What is Emotion? Histories, Measures, and Meanings* (New Haven, CT: Yale University Press, 2007).

Kahn, Jeffrey P. *Angst: Origins of Anxiety and Depression* (New York: Oxford University Press, 2013).

Karremans, Johan C., et al. "When Forgiving Enhances Psychological Well-Being: The Role of Interpersonal Commitment," *Journal of Personality and Social Psychology*, vol. 84, no. 5 (May 2003), pp. 1011-1026.

Kaskutas, Lee Ann. "Alcoholics Anonymous Effectiveness: Faith Meets Science," *Journal of Addictive Diseases*, vol. 28, no. 2 (April 2009), pp. 145-157.

Kaufman, Gordon D. *Jesus and Creativity* (Minneapolis: Fortress Press, 2006).

Kavanaugh, John F. *Following Christ in a Consumer Society* (Maryknoll, NY: Orbis Books, 1991).

Kaveny, M. Cathleen. "Billable Hours in Ordinary Time: A Theological Critique of the Instrumentalization of Time in Professional Life," *Loyola University Chicago Law Journal*, vol. 33, no. 1 (Fall 2001), pp. 173-220.

Kay, Aaron C., et al. "Randomness, Attributions of Arousal and Belief in God," *Psychological Science*, vol. 21, no. 2 (February 2010), pp. 216-218.

Kearney, Richard. *Strangers, Gods and Monsters* (London/New York: Routledge, 2003).

———. *Anatheism: Returning to God After God* (New York: Columbia University Press, 2010).

Keizer, Garret. *The Enigma of Anger: Essays on a Sometimes Deadly Sin* (San Francisco: Jossey-Bass, 2002).

Keller, Bill. "How to Die," *New York Times*, October 8, 2012, p. A21.

Keller, Timothy J. *Counterfeit Gods: The Empty Promises of Money, Sex, and Power, and the Only Hope That Matters* (New York: Dutton, 2009).

———. *The Reason for God: Belief in an Age of Skepticism* (New York: Riverhead Books, 2008).

Keltner, Dacher. *Born to Be Good: The Science of a Meaningful Life* (New York: W. W. Norton & Co., 2009).

Kenaan, Hagi. *The Present Personal: Philosophy and the Hidden Face of Language* (New York: Columbia University Press, 2005).

King, Gillian A., et al. *Resilience: Learning from People with Disabilities and the Turning Points in Their Lives* (Westport, CT: Praeger, 2003).

Klinkenborg, Verlyn. "Our Vanishing Night," *National Geographic*, vol. 214, no. 5 (November 2008), pp. 102-123.

Kluger, Jeffrey. *Simplexity: Why Simple Things Become Complex (and How Complex Things Can Be Made Simple)* (New York: Hyperion, 2008).

Kohák, Erazim V. *The Embers and the Stars: A Philosophical Inquiry into the Moral Sense of Nature* (Chicago: University of Chicago Press, 1984).

Kolakowski, Leszek. *Is God Happy? Selected Essays* (New York: Basic Books, 2013).

Konigsberg, Ruth Davis. *The Truth About Grief: The Myth of Its Five Stages and the New Science of Loss* (New York: Simon & Schuster, 2011). It is in ftn!

Krauss, Lawrence M. *A Universe from Nothing: Why There is Something Rather Than Nothing* (New York: Free Press, 2012).

Kugel, James L. *In the Valley of the Shadow: On the Foundations of Religious Belief* (New York: Free Press, 2011).

Kuhl, David. *What Dying People Want: Practical Wisdom for the End of Life* (New York: Public Affairs, 2002).

Kurzweil, Ray. *The Age of Spiritual Machines: When Computers Exceed Human Intelligence* (New York: Penguin, 1999).

Kushner, Harold S. *Why Bad Things Happen to Good People* (New York: Schocken Books, 1981).

⎯⎯⎯⎯. *How Good Do We Have to Be? A New Understanding of Guilt and Forgiveness* (Boston: Little, Brown and Company, 1997).

Labahn, Michael, and Bert Jan Lietaert Peerbolte, eds. *A Kind of Magic: Understanding Magic in the New Testament and Its Religious Environments* (New York: T & T Clark, 2007).

Lakoff, George. *Women, Fire, and Dangerous Things: What Categories Reveal about the Mind* (Chicago: University of Chicago Press, 1987).

Lamb, Sharon, and Jeffrie G. Murphy, eds. *Before Forgiving: Cautionary Views of Forgiveness in Psychotherapy* (place: 2002).

Lamott, Anne. *Help, Thanks, Wow: The Three Essential Prayers* (New York: Riverhead Books, 2012).

⎯⎯⎯⎯. *Grace (Eventually): Thoughts on Faith* (New York: Riverhead Books, 2007).

Larson, Edward J., and Larry Wiltham. "Leading Scientists Still Reject God," *Nature*, vol. 394, no. 6691 (July 23, 1998), p. 313.

Laughlin, Robert B. *A Different Universe: Reinventing Physics from the Bottom Down* (New York: Basic Books, 2005).

Leavy, Stanley A. *In the Image of God: A Psychoanalyst's View* (New Haven, Ct: Yale University Press, 1988).

Lederman, Leon, and Christopher Hill. *Beyond the God Particle* (Amherst, NY: Prometheus Books, 2013).

Leonard, Richard, SJ. *Where the Hell is God?* (Mahwah, NJ: HiddenSpring, 2010).

Levine, Robert. *A Geography of Time: The Temporal Misadventures of a Social Psychologist, or How Every Culture Keeps Time a Little Bit Differently* (New York: BasicBooks, 1997).

Levine, Stephen K. *Trauma, Tragedy, Therapy: The Arts and Human Suffering* (London: Jessica Kingsley Publishers, 2009).

⎯⎯⎯⎯. *Unattended Sorrow: Recovering from Loss and Reviving the Heart* (New York: Rodale, 2005).

Lieberman, Philip. *The Unpredictable Species: What Makes Humans Unique* (Princeton, NJ: Princeton University Press, 2013).

──────. *Toward an Evolutionary Biology of Language* (Cambridge, MA: Belknap Press of Harvard University, 2006).

Lightman, Alan. *The Accidental Universe: The World You Thought You Knew* (New York: Pantheon Books, 2013).

Livio, Mario. *Is God a Mathematician?* (New York: Simon and Schuster, 2009).

Long, James. *Why is God Silent When We Need Him the Most? A Journey of Faith into the Articulate Silence of God* (Grand Rapids: Zondervan, 1994).

Luhrman, T. M. *When God Talks Back: Understanding the American Evangelical Relationship with God* (New York: Alfred A. Knopf, 2012).

Lutz, Tom. *Crying: The Natural and Cultural History of Tears* (New York: W. W. Norton & Company, 1999).

Lynch, James L. *The Language of the Heart: The Human Body in Dialogue* (New York: Basic Books, Inc., 1985).

Mackenzie, Dana. *The Big Splat, or How Our Moon Came to Be* (New York: John Wiley & Sons, Inc., 2003).

Maisel, Eric. *Rethinking Depression: How to Shed Mental Health Illness and Create Personal Meaning* (Novato, CA: New World Library, 2012).

Majka, Frank, SJ. "What Didn't Jesus Say?," *Marquette Magazine* (Spring 2010), p. 48.

Malt, Barbara, and Phillip Wolf. *Words and the Mind: How Words Capture Human Experience* (Oxford: Oxford University Press, 2010).

Manoussakis, John P. *God After Metaphysics: A Theological Aesthetic* (Bloomington IN: Indiana University Press, 2007).

Marion, Jim. *The Death of the Mythic God: The Rise of Evolutionary Spirituality* (Charlottesville, VA: Hampton Roads Pub., 2004).

Martin, James, SJ. *Between Heaven and Mirth: Why Joy, Humor, and Laughter Are at the Heart of Spiritual Life* (New York: HarperOne, 2011).

Martin, Mike W. *Happiness and the Good Life* (New York: Oxford University Press, 2012).

Martin, Regis. *Still Point: Loss, Longing, and Our Search for God* (Notre Dame, IN: Ave Maria Press, 2012).

McCartin, James. *Prayers of the Faithful: The Shifting Spiritual Life of American Catholics* (Cambridge, MA: Harvard University Press, 2010).

McCauley, Robert N. *Why Religion is Natural and Science Is Not* (New York: Oxford University Press, 2011).

McCrea, Bridget. "Cancer Times Two," *cancerfightersthrive*, vol. 7, no. 16 (Summer 2012), pp. 8-10.

McCullough, Michael E. *Beyond Revenge: The Evolution of the Forgiveness Instinct* (San Francisco: Jossey-Bass, 2008).

McIntyre, Lee. *Dark Ages: The Case for a Science of Human Behavior* (Cambridge, MA: MIT Press, 2006).

McKim, Robert. "The Hiddenness of God," *Religious Studies*, vol. 26, no. 1 (March 1990), pp. 141-161.

McTaggart, J. Ellis. "The Unreality of Time," *Mind*, vol. 17, no. 68 (October 1908), pp. 457-474.

Menke, Cajetan J. *The Problem of Prayer: The Meaning and Value of Prayer in the Light of Certain Contemporary Theological Trends* (Toronto: St. Michael's College, Ph.D. dissertation, 1977).

Miles, Jack. *God: A Biography* (New York: Vintage Books, 1995).

Miller, Lisa. *Heaven: Our Enduring Fascination with the Afterlife* (New York: Harper, 2010).

Mlodinow, Leonard. *The Drunkard's Walk: How Randomness Rules Our Lives* (New York: Vintage Books, 2009).

Moär, Eli. *To Infinity and Beyond: A Cultural History of the Infinite* (Boston: Birkhauser, 1987).

Morris, Simon Conway. *Life's Solution: Inevitable Humans in a Lonely Universe* (Cambridge, UK/New York: Cambridge University Press, 2003).

Morrow, Lance. *Evil: An Investigation* (New York: Basic Books, 2003).

Mullainathan, Sendhil, and Eldar Shafir. *Scarcity: Why Having Too Little Means So Much* (New York: Times Books, Henry Holt and Company, 2003).

Naef, Rahel, and Debra A. Bournes. "The Lived Experience of Waiting," *Nursing Science Quarterly*, vol. 22, no. 2 (April 2009), pp. 141-153.

Nash, Richard. *John Craige's Mathematical Principles of Christian Theology* (Carbondale, IL: Southern Illinois University, 1991).

Needleman, Jacob. *Why Can't We Be Good?* (New York: Jeremy P. Tarcher/Penguin, 2007).

Newberg, Andrew B., et al. *Why God Won't Go Away: Brain Science and the Biology of Belief* (New York: Ballantine Books, 2001).

Nida, Eugene A. *God's Word in Man's Language* (New York Harper & Row Publishers, 1952).

Niedzviecki, Hal. *Hello, I'm Special: How Individuality Became the New Conformity* (San Francisco: City Lights Books, 2006).

Norenzayan, Ara. *Big Gods: How Religion Transformed Cooperation and Conflict* (Princeton and Oxford: Princeton University Press, 2013).

Nowak, Martin A., and Sarah Coakley. *Evolution, Games, and God: The Principle of Cooperation* (Cambridge, MA: Harvard University Press, 2013).

Numbers, Ronald L. *Galileo Goes to Jail and Other Myths about Science and Religion* (Boston: Harvard University Press, 2011).

Ofri, Danielle. *Medicine in Translation: Journeys with My Patients* (Boston: Beacon Press, 2010).

Ong, Walter, SJ. *Orality and Literacy: The Technologizing of the Word* (London/New York: Methuen, 1982).

Ouellette, Jennifer. *Me, Myself, and Why: Searching for the Science of Self* (New York: Penguin, 2014).

Overbye, Dennis. "There's More to Nothing Than We Knew," *New York Times*, January 21, 2012, pp. D1, D3.

Pais, Abraham. *Subtle is the Lord: The Science and Life of Albert Einstein* (Oxford: Oxford University Press, 1982).

Paulos, John Allen. *Irreligion: A Mathematician Explains Why the Arguments for God Just Don't Add Up* (New York: Hill and Wang, 2008).

Pennebaker, James W., and Sandra Klihr Beall. "Confronting a Traumatic Event: Toward an Understanding of Inhibition and Disease," *Journal of Abnormal Psychology*, vol. 95, no. 3 (August 1986), pp. 274-281.

Penrose, Roger. *Shadows of the Mind: A Search for the Missing Science of Consciousness* (Oxford/New York: Oxford University Press, 1994).

Pentman, Alex. *Social Physics: How Good Ideas Spread—The Lessons from a New Science* (New York: The Penguin Press, 2014).

Perakh, Mark. *Unintelligent Design* (Amherst, NY: Prometheus Books, 2004).

Perry, Ronen. "It's a Wonderful Life," *Cornell Law Review*, vol. 93, no. 2 (January 2008), pp. 329-399.

Persinger, Michael A. "The Neuropsychology of Paranormal Experiences," *Journal of Neuropsychiatry and Clinical Neuroscience*, vol. 13, no. 4 (Fall 2001), pp. 515-524.

Pesic, Peter. *Labyrinth: A Search for the Hidden Meaning of Science* (Cambridge, MA: MIT Press, 2000).

Pitchford, Susan R. *God in the Dark: Suffering and Desire in the Spiritual Life* (Collegeville, MN: Liturgical Press, 2011).

Plant, Sadie. *Zeroes and Ones: Digital Women and the New Technoculture* (New York: Doubleday, 1997).

Poe, Harry Lee, and Stanley Mattson, eds. *What God Knows: Time, Eternity, and Divine Knowledge* (Waco, TX: Baylor University Press, 2005).

Polkinghorne, John. *Science and Religion in Quest of Truth* (New Haven, CT: Yale University Press, 2011).

_____. *Quantum Physics and Theology: An Unexpected Kinship* (New Haven, CT/London: Yale University Press, 2007).

Powell, Corey S. "Darklands of the Cosmos," *Discover* (July-August 2013), pp. 90-92.

Prochnik, George. *In Pursuit of Silence: Listening for Meaning in a World of Noise* (New York: Doubleday, 2010).

Prothero, Stephen. *The American Bible: How Our Words Unite, Divide, and Define a Nation* (New York: HarperOne, 2012).

Quill, Timothy E. "Dying and Decision-Making—Evolution of End-of-Life Options," *New England Journal of Medicine*, vol. 350, no. 20 (May 13, 2004), pp. 2029-2032.

Raju, C. K. "The Religious Roots of Mathematics," *Theory, Culture and Society*, vol. 23, nos. 2-3 (2006), pp. 95-97.

Rakoff, Todd D. *A Time for Every Purpose: Law and the Balance of Life* (Cambridge, MA: Harvard University Press. 2002).

Randall, Lisa. *Knocking on Heaven's Door: How Physics and Scientific Thinking Illuminate the Universe and the Modern World* (New York: Ecco, 2011).

Rees, Martin. *Just Six Numbers: The Deep Forces That Shape the Universe* (New York: Basic, 2000).

Reid, Constance. *From Zero to Infinity: What Makes Numbers Interesting* (Wellesley, MA: Peters, 2006).

Reilly, Brendan, MD. *One Doctor: Close Calls, Cold Cases and the Mysteries of Medicine* (New York: Atria Books, 2013). Ck. Place.

Rescher, Nicholas *The Limits of Science* (Berkeley, CA: University of California Press, 1984).

Ribot, Théodule. *Les maladies de la mémoire* (Paris: Librairie Germer Balliere, et Cie, 1881).

Rizzuto, Ana-Maria. *The Birth of the Living God* (Chicago: University of Chicago Press, 1979).

Rohlheiser, Ronald. *The Holy Longing: The Search for a Christian Spirituality* (New York: Doubleday, 1999).

Rohr, Richard. *Falling Upward: A Spirituality for the Two Halves of Life* (San Francisco: Jossey-Bass, 2011).

Rosemont, Henry, and Huston Smith. *Is There a Universal Grammar of Religion?* (Chicago: Open Court, 2008).

Rosen, Larry D. *iDisorder: Understanding Our Obsession with Technology and Overcoming Its Hold on Us* (New York: Palgrave Macmillan, 2012).

Rosen, Steven. *Ultimate Journey: Death and Dying in the World's Major Religions* (Westport, CT: Praeger, 2008).

Rosenberg, Alexander. *The Atheist's Guide to Reality: Enjoying Life Without Illusions* (New York: W. W. Norton, 2011).

Rosenberg, Karen, "The Rich Detailed Fullness Found in Empty," *New York Times*, November 5, 2010, p. C35.

Rosenhahn, David L. "On Being Sane in Insane Places," *Science*, New Series, vol. 179, no. 4070 (January 1973), pp. 250-258.

Ross, Hugh. *The Fingerprint of God* (New Kensington, PA: Whitaker House, 2000).

Rothstein, Edward. *Emblems of Mind: The Inner Life of Music and Mathematics* (New York: Times Books/Random House, 1995).

Rushnell, Squire. *When God Winks at You: How God Speaks Directly to You through the Power of Coincidence* (Nashville: Nelson Books, 2006).

Russell, Robert John. "Does 'The God Who Acts' Really Act? New Approaches to Divine Action in Light of Science," *Theology Today*, vol. 54, no. 1 (April 1997), pp. 43-65.

Rutherford, Adam. *Creation: How Science Is Reinventing Itself* (New York: Current, 2013).

Sacks, Jonathan. *The Great Partnership* (London: Hodder & Stoughton, 2011).

Sambo, Chiara F., et al. "Knowing You Care: Effects of Perceived Empathy and Attachment Style on Pain Perception," *Pain*, vol. 151, issue 3 (December 2010), pp. 687-693.

Sanders, Barry. *Unsuspecting Souls: The Disappearance of the Human Being* (Berkeley: Counterpoint, 2009).

Sanford, John A. *Evil: The Shadow Side of Reality* (New York: Crossroad Publishing Company, 1981).

Scalia, Elizabeth. *Strange Gods: Unmasking the Idols in Everyday Life* (Notre Dame, IN: Ave Maria Press, 2013).

Scarry, Elaine. *The Body in Pain: The Making and Unmaking of the World* (New York/Oxford: Oxford University Press, 1985).

Schieman, Scott. "The Religious Role and the Sense of Personal Control," *Sociology of Religion*, vol. 69, no. 3 (Fall 2008), pp. 273-296.

Schoenstene, Robert. "Religion and Science," *Chicago Studies*, vol. 51, no. 2 (Summer 2012), pp. 189-202.

Schroeder, Gerald L. *The Hidden Face of God: How Science Reveals the Ultimate Truth* (New York/London: The Free Press. 2001).

Schultz, Valerie. "The Peculiar Grace of Failure," *America*, vol. 197, Issue 7 (September 17, 2007), pp. 23-25.

Schulz, Kathryn. *Being Wrong: Adventures in the Margin of Error* (New York: HarperCollins, 2011).

Schwartz, Barry. *The Paradox of Choice: Why More is Less* (New York: Ecco, 2004).

_____, and Kenneth Sharpe. *Practical Wisdom: The Right Way to Do the Right Thing* (New York: Riverhead Books, 2010).

Schweitzer, Peter P., ed. *Dividends of Kinship: Meanings and Uses of Social Relatedness* (London: Routledge, 2000).

Seife, Charles. *Zero: The Biography of a Dangerous Idea* (New York: Penguin Books, 2000).

Seligman, Martin E. P. *Flourish: A Visionary New Understanding of Happiness and Well-Being* (New York: Free Press, 2011).

Shariff, Azim F., and Ara Norenzayan. "God is Watching You: Priming God Concepts Increases Prosocial Behavior in an Anonymous Economic Game," *Psychological Science*, vol. 18, no. 9 (September 2007), pp. 803-809.

Shiffrin, Seana Valentine. "Wrongful Life, Procreative Responsibility, and the Significance of Harm," *Legal Theory*, vol. 5, no. 2 (June 1999), pp. 117-148.

Shipley, Joseph T. *In Praise of English: The Growth and Use of Language* (New York: Times Books, 1977).

Shlain, Leonard. *The Alphabet and the Goddess: The Conflict Between Word and Image* (New York: Viking, 1998).

Shulevitz, Judith. *The Sabbath World: Glimpses of a Different Order of Time* (New York: Random House, 2010).

Silvertown, Jonathan. *The Long and the Short of It: The Science of Life Span and Aging* (Chicago: University of Chicago Press, 2014).

Singer, Peter. *Rethinking Life and Death: The Collapse of Our Traditional Ethics* (New York: St. Martin's Press, 2011).

Skeel, David A., Jr., and William J. Stuntz. "Christianity and the (Modest) Rule of Law," *University of Pennsylvania Journal of Constitutional Law*, vol. 8, no. 4 (August 2006), pp. 809-839.

Skidelsky, Robert, and Edward Skidelsky. *How Much is Enough? Money and the Good Life* (New York: Other Press, 2012).

Skinner, Stephen. *Sacred Geometry: Deciphering the Code* (New York: Sterling Publishing, 2006).

Sloan, Richard P. *Blind Faith: The Unholy Alliance of Religion and Medicine* (New York: St. Martin's Press, 2006).

Smith, Jesse M. "Becoming an Atheist in America: Constructing Identity and Meaning from the Rejection of Theism," *Sociology of Religion*, vol. 72, no. 2 (Summer 2011), pp. 215-237.

Smith, Richard H. *The Joy of Pain: Schadenfreude and the Dark Side of Human Nature* (Oxford: Oxford University Press, 2013).

Sober, Elliott, and David Sloan Wilson. *Unto Others: The Evolution and Psychology of Unselfish Behavior* (Cambridge/London: Harvard University Press, 1998).

Solove, Daniel J. *Understanding Privacy* (Cambridge, MA: Harvard University Press, 2009).

Spilka, Bernard, et al. "The Concept of God: A Factor-Analytic Approach," *Review of Religious Research*, vol. 6, no. 1 (Fall 1964), pp. 20-35.

Spitzer, Robert. *New Proofs for the Existence of God: Contributions of Contemporary Physics and Philosophy* (Grand Rapids: William B. Eerdmans Pub., 2010).

Spring, Janis Abrahms, with Michael Spring. *How Can I Forgive You? The Courage to Forgive, the Freedom Not to* (New York: HarperCollins, 2004).

Sproul, R. C. *Not a Chance: The Myth of Chance in Modern Science and Cosmology* (Grand Rapids, MI: Baker Books, 1994).

Stark, Rodney. "Gods, Rivals, and the Moral Order," *Journal for theScientific Study of Religion*, vol. 40, no. 4 (December 2001), pp. 619-636.

Starkey, A. Denise. *The Shame That Lingers: A Survivor-Centered Critique of Catholic Sin-Talk* (New York: Peter Lang Publishing, 2009).

Steiner, Ralph. *In Pursuit of Clouds: Images and Metaphors* (Albuquerque, NM: University of New Mexico Press, 1985).

Stenger, Victor J. *Has Science Found God? The Latest Results in the Search for Purpose in the Universe* (Amherst, NY: Prometheus Books, 2003).

Sternberg, Robert. J. "A Triangular Theory of Love," *Psychological Review*, vol. 93, no. 2 (April 1986), pp. 119-135.

Stiglitz, Joseph E. *The Price of Inequality: How Today's Divided Society Endangers Our Future* (New York: W. W. Norton & Co., 2012).

Stivers, Richard. *Shades of Loneliness: Pathologies of a Technological Society* (Lanham, MD: Rowman & Littlefield, 2004).

Stone, Alex. *Fooling Houdini: Magicians, Mentalists, Math Geeks, and the Hidden Powers of the Mind* (New York: Harper, 2012).

Storr, Anthony. *Solitude: A Return to the Self* (New York: Free Press, 1988).

Strogatz, Steven. *The Joy of x: A Guided Tour of Math, From One to Infinity* (Boston: Houghton Mifflin Harcourt, 2012).

Susskind, Leonard, and George Hrabovsky. *The Theoretical Minimum: What You Need to Know to Start Doing Physics* (New York: Basic Books, 2013).

Sweet, Victoria. *God's Hotel: A Doctor, a Hospital, and a Pilgrimage to the Heart of Medicine* (New York: Riverhead Books, 2012).

Tavris, Carol. *Anger: The Misunderstood Emotion* (New York: Simon & Schuster, 1984).

Taylor, Mark C. *Moment of Complexity: Emerging Network Culture* (Chicago: University of Chicago, 2001).

Taylor, Rodney L. and Jean Watson. *They Shall Not Hurt: Human Suffering and Human Caring* (Boulder, CO: Colorado Association University Press, 1989).

Tenner, Edward. *Why Things Bite Back: Technology and the Revenge of Unintended Consequences* (New York: Knopf, 1996).

Thomas, J. L. H. "Why Did It Happen to Me?," *Religious Studies*, vol. 26, no. 3 (September 1990), pp. 323-347.

Tiger, Lionel, and Michael T. McGuire. *God's Brain* (Amherst, NY: Prometheus Books, 2010).

Tipler, Frank J. *Physics of Immortality: Modern Cosmology, God, and the Resurrection of the Dead* (New York: Doubleday, 1994).

Tomasello, Michael. *Why We Cooperate* (Cambridge, MA: MIT Press, 2009).

Trimble, Michael. *Why Humans Like to Cry: Tragedy, Evolution, and the Brain* (Oxford: Oxford University Press, 2012).

Trivers, Robert. *The Folly of Fools: The Logic of Deceit and Self-Deception in Human Life* (New York: Basic Books, 2011).

Tugend, Alina. "In a Data-Heavy Society, Being Defined by the Numbers," *New York Times*, April 23, 2011, p. B5.

Turkle, Sherry. *Alone Together: Why We Expect More from Technology and Less from Each Other* (New York: Basic Books, 2011).

Van Boven, Leaf, and Thomas Gilovich. "To Do or To Have: That is the Question," *Journal of Personality and Social Psychology*, vol. 85, no. 6 (December 2003), pp. 1193-1202.

Vanderkam, Laura. *All the Money in the World: What the Happiest People Know about Getting and Spending* (Place: Portfolio/Penguin, 2012).

Vertosick, Frank T. *Why We Hurt: The Natural History of Pain* (New York: Harcourt, 2000).

Wade, Nicholas. *The Faith Instinct: How Religion Evolved and How It Endures* (New York: The Penguin Press, 2009).

Walker, Gabrielle. *An Ocean of Air: Why the Wind Blows and Other Mysteries of the Atmosphere* (Orlando: Harcourt, 2007).

Wallis, Jim. *On God's Side: What Religion Forgets and Politics Hasn't Learned About Serving the Common Good* (Grand Rapids: Brazos Press, 2013).

Walters, Kerry. *Godlust: Facing the Demonic, Embracing the Divine* (New York: Paulist Press, 1999).

Ward, Keith. *God, Chance & Necessity* (Oxford: One World, 1996).

Wax, John. "The Inner Life: A New Dimension of Rehabilitation," *Journal of Rehabilitation*, vol. 38, no. 6 (November-December 1972), pp. 16-18.

Webb, Stephen H. *The Gifting God: A Trinitarian Ethics of Excess* (New York: Oxford, 1996).

Webb, Val. *Like Catching Water in a Net: Human Attempts to Describe the Divine* (New York/London: Continuum, 2007).

Welch, John, O. Carm. *The Carmelite Way: An Ancient Path for Today's Pilgrim* (Mahwah, NJ: Paulist Press, 1996).

Wertheim, Margaret. *The Pearly Gates of Cyberspace: A History of Space from Dante to the Internet* (New York: W. W. Norton, 1999).

Westen, Peter. "The Empty Idea of Equality," *Harvard Law Review*, vol. 95, no. 3 (January 1982), pp. 537-596.

Whitelaw, Ian. *A Measure of All Things: The Story of Man and Measurement* (New York: St. Martin's Press, 2007).

Wicks, Robert J. *Bounce: Living the Resilient Life* (New York: Oxford University Press, 2010).

Wilkinson, Richard G. *The Spirit Level: Why Greater Equality Makes Societies Stronger* (New York: Bloomsbury Press, 2009).

Wiman, Christian. *My Bright Abyss: Meditation of a Modern Believer* (New York: Farrar, Straus & Giroux, 2013).

Winter, Richard. *When Life Goes Dark: Finding Hope in the Midst of Depression* (Downers Grove, IL: IVP Books, 2012 ).

Wolpe, David. *Making Loss Matter: Creating Meaning in Difficult Times* (New York: Riverhead Books, 1999).

Wright, N. T. *After You Believe: Why Christian Character Matters* (New York: HarperOne, 2010).

Wright, Robert. *Nonzero: The Logic of Human Destiny* (New York: Pantheon Books, 2000).

Wulf, Andrea. *Chasing Venus: The Race to Measure the Heavens* (New York: Alfred A. Knopf, 2012).

Yancey, Philip. *Rumors of Another World: What on Earth Are We Missing?* (Grand Rapids, MI: Zondervan, 2003).

Yanofsky, Noson S. *The Outer Limits of Reason: What Science, Math, and Logic Cannot Tell Us* (Cambridge, MA/London: The MIT Press, 2013).

Zak, Paul J. *The Moral Molecule* (New York: Dutton, 2012).

Zee, Arthur. *Fearful Symmetry: The Search for Beauty in Modern Physics* (New York: Macmillan Publishing Company, 1986).

Zelizer, Viviana. *The Social Meaning of Money: Pin Money, Paychecks, Poor Relief, and Other Currencies* (New York: Basic Books, 1994).

Zerubavel, Eviatar. *Elephant in the Room: Silence and Denial in Everyday Life* (Oxford: Oxford University Press, 2006).

Zimbardo, Philip G. *The Lucifer Effect: Understanding How Good People Turn Evil* (New York: Random House, 2007).

Zimmer, Carl. *Evolution: Making Sense of Life* (Greenwood Village, CO: Roberts and Company Publishers, 2013).

Zuger, Abigail, MD. "Resilience, Not Misery, in Coping with Loss," *New York Times*, December 29, 2009, p. D5.